INSIDE FORENSIC SCIENCE

Forensic Medicine

INSIDE FORENSIC SCIENCE

Forensic Medicine

Howard C. Adelman, M.D.

SERIES EDITOR | Lawrence Kobilinsky, Ph.D.

CHELSEA HOUSE
PUBLISHERS
An imprint of Infobase Publishing

To my many mentors (too numerous to mention) in medicine,
pathology, and forensic pathology, of whom a few stand out:
my Professors Gerhard Wolf-Heidegger, Jürg Im Obersteg,
Siegfried Scheidegger, Andreas Wertemann, Rudolf Nissen;
Drs. Irving Chapman, John Devlin, Sidney Weinberg; . . .
and most of all: Die Universität Basel—Medizinische Fakultät
(The University of Basel, Switzerland – School of Medicine).

Forensic Medicine

Copyright © 2007 by Infobase Publishing

Chelsea House
An imprint of Infobase Publishing
132 West 31st Street
New York, NY 10001

Library of Congress Cataloging-in-Publication Data

Adelman, Howard C.
    Forensic medicine / Howard C. Adelman.
        p. cm. — (Inside forensic science)
    Includes bibliographical references and index.
    ISBN-13: 978-0-7910-8926-2
    ISBN 0-7910-8926-6 (hardcover)
    1. Forensic pathology. I. Title.
RA1063.4.A34 2006
614'.1—dc22   2006020617

Text design and composition by Annie O'Donnell
Cover design by Ben Peterson
Cover printed by Yurchak Printing, Landisville, Pa.
Book printed and bound by Yurchak Printing, Landisville, Pa.

Printed in the United States of America

Table of Contents

Introduction: The Role of the Forensic Pharmacologist

Today, through television, most Americans have been exposed to the application of **forensic science** to the justice system. Programs such as *Law and Order*, *CSI*, *Crossing Jordan*, *Cold Case Files*, *Forensic Files*, and *American Justice* feature police activities, forensic laboratory technology, and courtroom procedures. These programs have made the public aware of the important role that forensic science plays in the criminal justice system, and enrollment in criminal justice and forensic science courses in college and high school has increased markedly within the last 10 years.

As a result of increased exposure to the work of forensic scientists, juror selection has become more difficult, since jurors now expect prosecutors to provide evidence as easily and as rapidly as seen on television. In selecting a jury panel, lawyers are aware that these television programs may influence jurors (called the "CSI effect") and the absence of expected evidence might work against the prosecutor in criminal cases.

Public attention is also drawn to the death of celebrities resulting from **drug** overdose. For example, Janis Joplin, the blues singer, overdosed on heroin, actor River Phoenix and comedian

John Belushi both overdosed on speedballs, a mixture of heroin and cocaine, and college basketball star Len Bias and Cleveland Browns football player Don Rogers both overdosed on cocaine.

Have you ever wondered how scientists determine whether a drug was involved in a particular case, and whether the amount of drug is considered an overdose and thus was the cause of death? Today many job applicants must submit a pre-employment urine sample to test for the presence of drugs, and random urine tests are performed on many individuals in high-stress jobs, including police officers, firefighters, pilots, and truck drivers. Have you wondered how such tests are performed to determine presence and quantity of drug? Are you curious to learn why alcohol is detected in breath samples? All of these issues fall under the broad heading of forensic science.

WHAT IS FORENSIC SCIENCE?

Forensic science can be defined as the application of science to legal issues. The role of science in resolving legal matters has increased substantially over the last 50 years. During this period, major advances in technology and information gathering have been made in the areas of medicine, molecular biology, analytical chemistry, computer science, and microscopy. Because the information and methodologies in these areas of science are so vast and complex, the law has become dependent on testimony by scientists to help unravel complex legal cases involving biological and physical evidence. Areas of science that may require explanation by experts include **pharmacology**, the study of all effects of chemicals on living organisms, and **toxicology**, the study of the toxic or adverse effects of chemicals, which are both the subjects of this book. There are other areas that require expert testimony, including DNA analysis, forensic medicine (anatomy and **pathology**), forensic odontology

FIGURE 1.1   Pharmacologist Dr. Donald H. Catlin sits in front of an LC/MS/MS system, an instrument used for detecting drugs from urine samples, at the UCLA Olympic Analytical Laboratory. Catlin is noted for developing a breakthrough test that detects the illegal steroid, tetrahydrogestrinone (THG), taken by athletes to enhance performance.

(dentistry), criminalistics (analysis of physical evidence such as hair, fibers, blood, paint, glass, soil, arson-related chemicals, and solid drug samples), questioned document examination (analysis of inks and papers), forensic engineering (accident reconstruction, environmental and construction analysis), firearm and toolmark analysis, forensic anthropology (analysis of bodily remains), forensic entomology (analysis of insects on deceased individuals to determine time of death), forensic psychology, voice pattern analysis, fingerprint analysis, and forensic nursing (effects of sexual assault and trauma).

A **pharmacologist** is a scientist who, in addition to being trained in the principles of pharmacology, studies other disciplines, including physiology, biochemistry, chemistry, molecular biology, statistics, and pathology, and usually possesses a Ph.D. degree (Figure 1.1). Pharmacology programs require a minimum of four years of graduate study, including a doctoral dissertation of original research. Chemicals studied by a pharmacologist may be natural (from plants or animals) or synthetic, and may include medicinals, drugs of abuse, poisons, carcinogens, and industrial chemicals. The pharmacologist must understand how chemicals interact with the most basic cell components such as receptors and DNA, and must explain how such interactions produce the observed results. The pharmacologist studies chemicals for their beneficial or therapeutic effects as well as their adverse or toxic effects. A **toxicologist**, usually someone with a Ph.D. degree, uses the same principles of science as the pharmacologist but generally studies only toxic or adverse effects of chemicals. Others working in a pharmacology or toxicology laboratory often have master or bachelor of science degrees in various specialties and are trained in experimentation and analytical procedures.

One of the basic principles of toxicology is that chemicals that are safe in appropriate doses can become toxic in higher doses. Even too much water can become toxic. Pharmacologists and toxicologists rely on dose-response tests, in which the effects of drugs are measured at different doses to see the relationship between dose and effect and, as the dosage increases, how the effect can quickly go from no effect to a desired effect to a toxic effect level. When studying chemicals, it is important to keep in mind a phrase of the famous fifteenth-century alchemist and physician Paracelsus (born Theophrastus Philippus Aureolus Bombastus von Hohenheim): "Is there anything that is not a poison? Everything is poison, and nothing is without poison. The dose alone makes a thing poisonous."[1]

This book will focus on forensic pharmacology and drugs of abuse. Drugs of abuse, such as cocaine, heroin, marijuana, PCP, benzodiazepines, and methamphetamine, are often involved in criminal and civil matters concerning personal injury, motor vehicle accidents, drug overdose, and murder, and thus, are discussed to illustrate forensic pharmacology issues and investigations.

What is forensic pharmacology and how does it differ from forensic toxicology? Both disciplines attempt to answer the question of whether a chemical was causally related to an individual's behavior, illness, injury, or death. The effect of the chemical might occur soon after exposure (an acute effect) or a long time after exposure (a chronic effect). To establish what caused the effect, scientists examine bodily tissues and fluids for the presence of drugs and, using different analytical techniques, identify chemicals and determine their concentration. Besides the obvious fluids of blood and urine, analysis can be performed on nails, hair, bone, semen, amniotic fluid, stomach contents, breast milk, **vitreous humor** (the fluid inside the eyeball), sweat, and saliva. What fluids and tissues are analyzed depends on the type of case and whether the subject is alive or deceased. Understanding of the chemical's **pharmacodynamics**, the mechanisms that bring about physiological and pathological changes, and **pharmacokinetics,** how the chemical is absorbed, distributed, metabolized, and excreted, are important in establishing a causal relationship. For example, once the concentration of a chemical and its **metabolites** in blood and/or urine are determined, it might be possible to determine when the drug was administered or taken. Interpretation of the findings, in relation to other facts and evidence in the case, may help solve a crime. On occasion, any items at a crime scene that may be drug related, such as syringes or vials containing a solution, are also brought to the forensic laboratory for analysis.

FORENSIC SCIENTISTS AT WORK

Most often, pharmacologists conduct research programs while employed in private, government, and commercial research laboratories, hospitals, and academic institutions. A pharmacologist may be contacted by an attorney and asked to consult or testify as an **expert witness** in legal matters that may be either criminal or civil and for the **plaintiff** or **defendant** (Figure 1.2). Attorneys learn of expert witnesses from advertisements in legal newspapers and journals, and by calling referral agencies that maintain lists of specialists in areas of medicine, science, engineering, finance, construction, aviation, and so on.

Interpretation of chemical data obtained from analysis of bodily fluids and tissues by a pharmacologist may help attorneys

FIGURE 1.2 In the photograph above, Dr. Jo Ellen Dyer, a pharmacist and toxicologist who specializes in GHB and sexual assault, serves as an expert witness at the rape trial of Max Factor heir, Andrew Luster. In 2003, Luster was convicted of raping a series of women after he used GHB, a "date rape" drug, to seduce his victims.

determine the role of a drug in an individual's behavior or death. If, for example, analysis shows a deceased person was under the influence of drugs, such data along with other facts in the case may help determine if death was due to an accidental overdose, suicide, or homicide by poisoning. In murder cases, it is important to know whether the deceased was under the influence of drugs. The prosecutor is interested, since it may explain the behavior of the deceased just before death, and the results may suggest to the defense attorney that a defendant charged with murder could have acted in self-defense. In civil lawsuits resulting from motor vehicle accidents or injuries from falls, whether those involved were under the influence of drugs may be an important factor.

The forensic pharmacologist will first review analytic reports to determine whether the data support the attorney's position. The review will focus on the positive aspects as well as on any areas that may be problematic in the case. The findings are presented to the attorney along with information that will help the attorney understand the science. If the pharmacologist's opinion is supportive, the attorney may request a written report. In many civil lawsuits, the use of experts results in settlements rather than trials. If the case goes to trial and the pharmacologist is expected to testify, the pharmacologist will assist the attorney in preparing a proper examination so that the testimony presented to the jury will be a clear and understandable explanation of the findings. Finally, the pharmacologist may assist the attorney in preparing a cross-examination of the opposing side's expert witness.

Forensic toxicologists are generally employed by federal, state, and local government crime laboratories, which may be affiliated with the medical examiner's office from which they receive fluids and tissues for analysis. They often work on criminal cases and usually testify for the office of the district attorney, the prosecutor. Forensic toxicologists may also be involved in drug testing in

History of Pharmacology and Toxicology

The science of pharmacology began with Rudolf Buchheim, a German pharmacologist who lived between 1820 and 1879. At the University of Dorpat in Russia (now Tartu in Estonia), he built a laboratory and began a systematic study of drug action. A pupil of Buchheim, Oswald Schmiedeberg succeeded Buchheim at Dorpat in 1866. Later, Schmiedeberg moved to Strasbourg, France, and developed a very successful program in pharmacology. Students came from all over the world. One of the students was John Jacob Abel, who then returned to the United States and became chairman of the first pharmacology department in a medical school, at the University of Michigan, in 1891. Abel is considered the father of American pharmacology, and played a major role in the organization of the American Society for Pharmacology and Experimental Therapeutics (ASPET). Today, pharmacology is part of the educational programs at medical, nursing, pharmacy, and other health professional schools.

Some of the earliest forensic toxicologists were Alexander Gettler, Raymond Abernethy, and Rutherford Gradwohl. In their time, analytical instruments and procedures were in their infancy, but they developed many of the techniques used today in chemical analysis. They were founders of the American Academy of Forensic Sciences (AAFS) in 1948. Today, the AAFS is divided among 10 sections: criminalistics, engineering sciences, general, jurisprudence, odontology, pathology/biology, physical anthropology, psychiatry and behavioral sciences, questioned documents, and toxicology.

the workplace or in sports. The pharmacologist may be involved in a broader scope of forensic issues than the toxicologist, with such diverse cases as adverse drug reactions to medicines, overdose of medicines, drug interactions, personal injury following exposure to medicines, effects from drugs of abuse or industrial chemicals, and induction of cancer by chemicals.

REAL-LIFE CASES

One of the authors has testified in court as an expert witness on many drug-related issues, including unexpected reactions to a medicine, whether a person accused of assault or murder of an attacker who had high blood levels of drugs of abuse could reasonably claim self-defense, whether exposure to medicinal chemicals, industrial chemicals, mercury-containing herbal preparations, carbon monoxide, or lead paint could have caused certain injuries or illnesses, whether drugs could have affected the behavior of people involved in motor vehicle accidents or accused of murder, and whether the presence of drugs of abuse in urine can be explained by reasons other than intentional drug abuse. Examples from these actual forensic pharmacology cases will be presented in the individual drug chapters.

As an example of an actual criminal case, two defendants were accused of raping a woman they had invited to their apartment. They claimed that the victim drank herself into a stupor within about 30 minutes after arrival, that she imagined the rape occurred, and that she left on her own about four hours later. The victim testified that she had two beers and one scotch within a 2.5-hour period. At some point she excused herself to make a phone call. Shortly after she returned and finished her drink, she felt dizzy and lost consciousness. She awoke briefly to find herself being raped but was weak, in a dreamlike state, and could not speak or move. She was able to leave about two hours later with the assistance of family members. The author's testimony before the jury explained that the amount of alcohol consumed by the victim was insufficient to induce unconsciousness and that if enough alcohol had been consumed to reach a level of unconsciousness, as the defendants claimed, given the rate of alcohol metabolism, it is highly unlikely a person would appear relatively normal several hours later. The author's opinion was that when the victim left the room to make the phone call, it is likely that drugs were added to her drink. This testimony, along with other evidence, helped the jury find the two defendants guilty, and they were sentenced to up to 25 years in prison.

As an example of an actual civil case not involving drugs of abuse, an infant developed seizures after being hospitalized for fever. Analysis of the infant's bodily fluids revealed the presence of high levels of theophylline, a drug used to treat asthma that in high doses can cause seizures. The plaintiff alleged that an error occurred in the hospital and that the infant was given theophylline instead of an antibiotic. At trial, the hospital countered that the theophylline in the infant came from the mother's breast milk, since the mother was taking theophylline for asthma and was breast-feeding her child. Theophylline pharmacokinetic data were presented to the jury indicating that the amount of theophylline excreted via breast milk could never account for the levels found in the infant. An error in drug administration probably occurred. The parties settled the lawsuit.

This book will outline what forensic pharmacology is and how it is used in similar cases in the real world. Chapter 2 will describe principles used by forensic pharmacologists to establish causation, namely pharmacokinetics and pharmacodynamics. Chapter 3 will describe the tools used by forensic scientists to identify and quantify chemicals in bodily fluids and tissues. Chapter 4 will describe current trends in drug abuse, focusing on drug abuse by adolescents. Chapters 5 to 12 will describe the pharmacology of eight major categories of drugs of abuse as well as interesting forensic issues for many of the drugs. Chapter 13 will discuss the future of forensic pharmacology, and Chapter 14 will test the reader's knowledge by presenting several cases for the reader to solve. There are hundreds of street names for many of the drugs of abuse. We have selected a few names from select resources for each drug, and the bibliography and further reading list should be consulted for additional references.

2

Pharmacokinetics and Pharmacodynamics

The first aspect of pharmacokinetics involves the entry of a drug into the body. Chemicals, in the form of foods, medicines, drugs of abuse, or industrial chemicals, can enter the human body via several routes, including ingestion, inhalation, injection, skin application, and suppository. Except for cases of injection directly into the bloodstream, the chemical must pass through complex living cell membranes before it can enter the bloodstream.

For example, chemicals that enter the digestive tract must be absorbed by the cells lining the small intestine and then be transferred through the cells, where the chemical can then be absorbed by the capillary cells into the bloodstream. Chemicals that are inhaled must pass through the **alveoli,** the cells of the lungs, to get to the capillaries and enter the bloodstream.

As chemicals pass into and out of cells, they must cross the cell membrane that keeps all of the cell contents securely inside, but which allows some materials to pass (Figure 2.1). Chemicals can move through the cell membrane through one of several mechanisms.

One of the mechanisms for moving chemicals through the cell membrane is passive **diffusion**, which is based on the difference

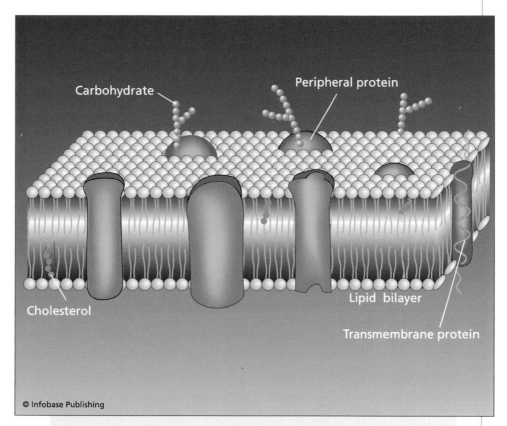

Carbohydrate

Peripheral protein

Cholesterol

Lipid bilayer

Transmembrane protein

© Infobase Publishing

FIGURE 2.1 The cell membrane consists mainly of lipids (fats), proteins, and carbohydrates in the form of a lipid bilayer. The two lipid layers face each other inside the membrane, and the water-soluble phosphate groups of the membrane face the watery contents inside the cell (the cytoplasm) and outside the cell (the interstitial fluid).

in concentration of the chemical outside of the cell compared to inside the cell. The greater the difference, the greater the movement of the chemical to the inside of the cell. Since the membrane is highly lipid in nature, **lipophilic** (lipid-loving) chemicals will diffuse more easily across the membrane. Ionized molecules that are more water soluble do not diffuse across membranes as readily as lipophilic molecules and are influenced by the **pH** of the fluid surrounding the cell. Water-soluble chemicals can also be transported using carrier proteins, and this process is called facilitated diffusion.

Inorganic ions, such as sodium and potassium, move through the cell membrane by active transport. Unlike diffusion, energy is required for active transport as the chemical is moving from a lower concentration to a higher one. One example is the sodium-potassium ATPase pump, which transports sodium $[Na^+]$ ions out of the cell and potassium $[K^+]$ into the cell.

Chemicals may cross the cell membrane via membrane pores. This diffusion depends on the size of the pore and the size and weight of the chemical. The chemical flows through the membrane along with water. Finally, the membrane can actually engulf the chemical, form a small pouch called a vesicle, and transport it across the membrane to the inside of the cell. This process is called pinocytosis.

DISTRIBUTION OF CHEMICALS

Once the chemical is in the bloodstream, it can be distributed to various organs. Initially its concentration in blood is greater than in tissues. Because of the difference in concentration, the chemical will leave the blood and enter the surrounding cells.

Sometimes other factors affect the movement of the chemical. For example, not all chemicals easily enter the brain. The capillary cells in the brain have tight junctions restricting the flow of materials between cells. One type of cell forms a tight covering on the capillary and prevents or slows down large molecules from passing through the cells. This structure is known as the **blood-brain barrier**. All of the drugs discussed in this book—drugs of abuse—affect the **central nervous system (CNS)**, which consists of the brain and spinal cord. Thus, the drug must pass through the blood-brain barrier.

The availability of a chemical to the cells is affected by where it is stored. First, lipophilic chemicals tend to get absorbed by and retained in fat cells, from which they are released slowly back into the bloodstream. Second, some chemicals are strongly bound to plasma proteins and are released to the cells more slowly over time. For example, acetaminophen (Tylenol®) does not bind strongly to plasma proteins, while diazepam (Valium®) does. Thus, diazepam will persist in the body for longer periods of time than will acetaminophen. Finally, some elements, such as fluorine, lead, and strontium, are bound up in bone for long periods of time. As bone slowly renews itself or is broken down under special circumstances such as pregnancy, the chemicals are released and can affect the mother and fetus.

METABOLISM OF CHEMICALS

Many **xenobiotics**, or chemicals that are foreign to the body, undergo metabolism. This type of metabolism is different from the metabolism of food nutrients necessary for production of energy to drive bodily functions. The purpose of xenobiotic metabolism is to convert active chemicals into inactive forms or convert inactive chemicals into active ones, and to transform chemicals into more water-soluble forms so that they can be more easily excreted via the urine and bile. To understand drug action, it is important to know whether the original chemical or the product of its metabolism (its metabolites), or both, is responsible for the pharmacological effects.

While many tissues can metabolize foreign chemicals, metabolism of xenobiotics primarily occurs in the liver. It is important to note that everything that is ingested and passes into the intestine first passes through the liver before entering the general circulation. Thus, you can think of the liver as the filter for the entire body.

Metabolism of xenobiotics proceeds via a two-stage process. Phase I consists of oxidation, reduction, or hydrolysis to form polar groups such as hydroxyl (OH) or carboxyl (COOH). Phase II consists of conjugation, whereby enzymes add to the polar groups glucuronic acid, sulfate, acetate, or glutathione, making the chemical more water soluble. Sometimes, the new metabolite is as active or more active than the parent chemical. Such an example is morphine-6-**glucuronide**, which is as active as morphine.

Phase I enzymes, located in the **endoplasmic reticulum**, include cytochrome P450-dependent monooxygenases. There are many genes for the different cytochrome P450 (CYP) enzymes, each acting on different sets of chemicals. Another Phase I enzyme, monoamine oxidase (MAO), can be found in mitochondria. The enzymes involved in Phase II metabolism are found mainly in the cytoplasm. Also in the cytoplasm is the enzyme alcohol dehydrogenase that metabolizes ethanol (drinking alcohol) to acetaldehyde which is then metabolized to acetic acid. Interestingly, exposure to the xenobiotic chemical sometimes increases the amount of the enzyme used for its own metabolism.

Since one particular enzyme system can metabolize many different chemicals, there is great potential for drug interaction. If one drug can increase the level of a specific enzyme, a second drug metabolized by that enzyme would also be more quickly metabolized. This may result in enhanced activity or a lowering of the drug's blood level and decreased effectiveness of one or both drugs. Also, if two drugs compete for an enzyme's activity, each drug might be metabolized more slowly, thereby prolonging their effects. Such information may be important in legal cases involving toxic effects of chemicals as a result of drug interaction.

Some people are rapid metabolizers of drugs and some are slow metabolizers. Factors that can affect the response to drugs include age, gender, and genetics. Very young children and older people metabolize drugs more slowly. There are some differences seen between men and women, as well as between races, in the metabolism of certain drugs. A new field of pharmacogenomics studies the role of genes in drug action and will someday allow for study of an individual's genes to determine in advance the response to drug therapy.

It is important to know how much of the chemical is destroyed as it passes through the liver to enter the general circulation. If, for example, someone ingests 100 milligrams of drug A and only 50 milligrams exits from the liver, then 50% of the drug was lost. This is known as the first-pass effect. Using this example, if 200 milligrams is required for a therapeutic effect, then a pharmaceutical manufacturer must incorporate 400 milligrams into each tablet. First-pass metabolism influences the effects of several drugs of abuse.

EXCRETION OF CHEMICALS

Chemicals and/or their metabolites are eventually eliminated. The three organs predominantly involved in elimination are the liver, the lungs, and the kidneys. Other routes of excretion include bile, feces, sweat, saliva, breast milk, nails, and hair.

As blood passes through the lungs for exchange of carbon dioxide and oxygen, volatile chemicals such as alcohol exit from the blood and are exhaled. Drugs that are eliminated via the bile are excreted into the small intestine and then eliminated via the feces, though some drugs are partly reabsorbed. This pattern of circulation, called enterohepatic circulation, from bile to intestine and back to liver, continues until the drug is completely eliminated. Blood is filtered as it passes through the kidney, and chemicals can leave the blood to become part of the urine forming in the renal tubules.

As a result of metabolism and excretion, drugs leave the body at certain rates. The rate of elimination may vary widely with different drugs, which explains why some medications must be taken four times daily, while others are taken only once a day. The **half-life** of a drug is the time in which the concentration of drug, generally in blood or **plasma**, decreases by 50%. Thus, if drug X has a half-life of three hours, and after absorption of drug X the blood concentration is 100 units, then three hours later the concentration would be 50 units, and three hours after that the blood concentration would be 25 units. After five half-lives, the concentration of drug X would be approximately 3% of the initial value. To maintain therapeutic levels of drug X, you might require taking a dose every three hours. Knowledge of excretion patterns of a chemical and of its metabolites is important for determining treatment schedules as well as for determining, in criminal or civil matters, when a drug had been taken or administered.

PHARMACODYNAMICS

Pharmacodynamics is the study of the mechanisms of drug action. How does a chemical cure disease, stimulate or inhibit the nervous system, change behavior, influence our digestive system, or induce a toxic reaction? The body itself is made up of chemicals, and when drugs (chemicals) are taken, the drugs interact with the body's chemicals and these interactions result in biochemical and physiological effects. While there are many different mechanisms of drug action that account for the different effects of diverse drugs, in this book we will restrict our discussion to those reactions that explain the effects of drugs of abuse. Drugs of abuse bring about their effects by interacting with cell receptors or by influencing the levels of various neurotransmitters, outlined below.

Cell Receptors

A receptor is a macromolecule on or in a cell with which a drug can interact and begin a sequence of events eventually leading to an effect. There are many receptors, some specific to a tissue or organ and others that are found more generally. Receptors include enzymes, regulatory proteins, and DNA-binding proteins. Often, the first reaction between chemical and receptor brings about a chain of reactions before the final effect is

The Science of Anatomy

The study of anatomy was originally restricted to animals. In the fourteenth century, an Italian named Mondino de' Liucci performed human dissection and published his findings. Leonardo da Vinci, born in the fifteenth century, was recognized as a painter, a scientist, and an engineer. His most famous paintings are the *Mona Lisa* and *The Last Supper*. Da Vinci was also interested in human anatomy and published the first textbook on human anatomy. Andreas Vesalius, a physician, was influenced by da Vinci's work. Vesalius published a seven-volume collection detailing the human body entitled *De Humani Corporis Fabrica*. In the eighteenth century, medical students were allowed to perform human dissection. In England, in 1858, Dr. Henry Gray published his first book, entitled *Anatomy, Descriptive and Surgical*. Today, many people know this book as *Gray's Anatomy*. In 1989, Frank H. Netter, a physician and medical illustrator, published his extremely detailed anatomical drawings in full color, termed *Atlas of Human Anatomy*.

produced. Drugs that bring about effects are called agonists. Chemicals that can block effects are termed antagonists.

Neuronal Signaling

At the end of each neuron are stores of chemicals called neurotransmitters that can be released to stimulate adjacent neurons (Figure 2.2). There are many different neurotransmitters, dependent on location and specific function in the nervous system. Generally, once a neuron is stimulated, the stimulus travels along the neuronal axon until it reaches the end of the neuron from which a neurotransmitter is released. The neurotrans-

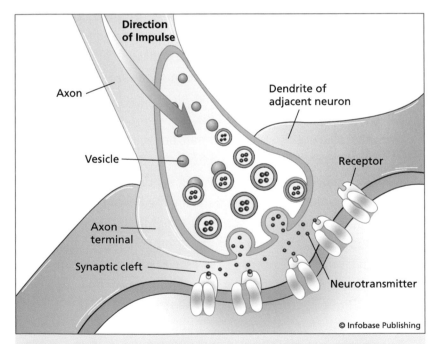

FIGURE 2.2   In this illustration of neuronal signaling, an electrical impulse causes the release of neurotransmitters from vesicles in the axon terminal of a neuron. The neurotransmitters cross the synapse (also known as the synaptic cleft) and bind to receptors on a receiving neuron.

mitter enters a space between the neuron it was released from and adjacent neurons. This space is called a synapse. The neurotransmitter diffuses across the synapse and excites a receptor on an adjacent neuron. Any chemical that has not attached itself to the surrounding neurons can either be destroyed by enzymes or be taken back up into the original neuron. Drugs can affect the function of the nervous system in several ways. They can stimulate or inhibit release of neurotransmitter, block its effects or affect its metabolism, prevent reuptake of the neurotransmitter, or mimic the effects of a neurotransmitter. Some examples of neurotransmitters in the CNS affected by drugs of abuse include gamma-aminobutyric acid (GABA), norepinephrine and dopamine, serotonin, endorphins, dynorphins, and enkephalins, and glutamate.

- Gamma-aminobutyric acid (GABA), is present in many areas of the brain, and is inhibitory. GABA can influence sensation of pain and affects memory, mood, and coordination. GHB and benzodiazepines increase GABA activity.

- Norepinephrine and dopamine are stimulants and increase mental alertness. Amphetamines activate norepinephrine receptors and also release norepinephrine and dopamine from storage; cocaine blocks the reuptake of dopamine.

- Serotonin (5HT) affects sleep, temperature, sexual behavior, sensory perception, appetite, and mood. There are many serotonin receptors, and activation of each brings about different effects. LSD and psilocybin activate serotonin receptors.

- Endorphins, dynorphins, and enkephalins are natural peptide neurotransmitters that activate the opioid receptors and affect sensation of pain, and induce **euphoria**, a feeling of well-being or elation.

- Glutamate activates the N-methyl-D-aspartate (NMDA) receptor. Glutamate is involved in perception of pain, sensory input, and memory. PCP and dextromethorphan block this receptor.

- The enzyme MAO metabolizes some of the neurotransmitters affected by some drugs of abuse, namely epinephrine, norepinephrine, dopamine, and serotonin. Dangerously high levels can result if an inhibitor of this enzyme, or **monoamine oxidase inhibitor** (**MAOI**), is used along with the drug of abuse.

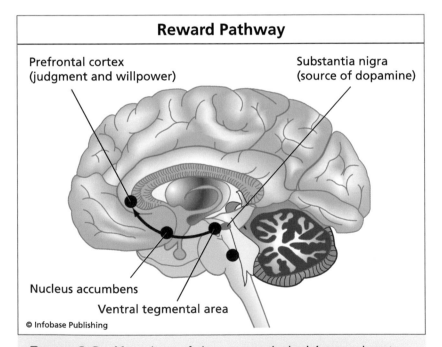

FIGURE 2.3 Many drugs of abuse act on the brain's reward center, which is illustrated above. The drugs cause neurons in the ventral tegmental area to release dopamine. The dopamine, in turn, initiates a chain of events that results in feelings of enjoyment and pleasure.

Many of the effects of drugs of abuse have been localized to what is termed the brain's reward center (Figure 2.3). The drugs increase the concentration of the neurotransmitter dopamine in the mesolimbic dopaminergic system. This system includes those areas of the brain designated as the ventral tegmental area (VTA), which transmits signals to the nucleus accumbens, prefrontal cortex, and other areas of the brain. All together these are considered the reward and drug seeking areas of the brain.

SUMMARY

The cell membrane is a complex structure of lipid, protein, and carbohydrate and regulates chemical passage via several mechanisms. Chemicals can interact with cell membranes or be absorbed into a cell to exert their pharmacologic effects. Chemicals reach their target via the bloodstream, and intracellular concentration is dependent on the extent of plasma protein binding. Most chemicals undergo some form of metabolism to be either activated or inactivated, or, in some cases, both. Lipid-soluble molecules tend to be deposited in fat cells and are released slowly over time. Eventually, chemicals are eliminated, most often via urine and feces. Drugs of abuse bring about their effects by interacting with cell receptors or by influencing the levels of various neurotransmitters.

3

Goals and Purpose of the Investigation

Once the postmortem interval has been evaluated, the next task of the forensic pathologist is to determine the identity of the deceased. It is not enough to find a Social Security card, a photographic driver's license, or even a passport on the person of the deceased. These items are only regarded as **presumptive identification**. A positive identification must be made.

A positive identification usually occurs when a friend, relative, or acquaintance of the deceased views the body and confirms the identity. However, in cases where the body is badly decomposed, mutilated by extensive trauma, or burned beyond recognition, other methods must be employed. The first task is to investigate any clues either on the person of the deceased, such as a driver's license, or in the environment (such as in an apartment), to determine the presumptive identification of the deceased. From this point, other experts may be consulted. A forensic dentist (**forensic odontologist**, from the Greek *odous* and the Latin *dens* = "tooth") can examine and x-ray the teeth of the deceased and compare them with the x-rays and the examinations made by the deceased's local dentist. If they match, shape for shape, filling for filling, missing or chipped tooth for missing or chipped tooth, the identity is confirmed. Fingerprinting is useful only if the deceased has his or her fingerprints on file in a national or local database.

DNA (**deoxyribonucleic acid**) is a nucleic acid found inside of the nucleus (from the Latin *nuculeus, nucleus* = "kernel," or *nucula* ="little nut") of all living cells. Outside of the nucleus is the remaining part of the cell called the cytoplasm, which can be used for identification only if there is a known specimen or family members with which to compare. DNA contains all of the genetic material unique to an individual, plant, or animal. This is the reason that DNA has often been referred to as a "genetic fingerprint."

Other soft evidence for presumptive identification includes the description of the clothes the deceased was last seen wearing, or personal items such as jewelry and other possessions.

In extreme cases, where only a skeletal remains is found, a **forensic anthropologist** (from the Greek *anthropikos* = "human being") can help determine the age, sex, race, and approximate height of the individual (Figure 3.1). A physical anthropologist or a sculptor trained in facial reconstruction can usually model a fairly accurate face from a skull, guessing at such things as eye color and hair (color, length, texture, or even the absence of it) on the scalp and face. After the reconstructed face is photographed from various sides and published, often someone will recognize the person and come forward with a presumptive identification, which then must be confirmed.

DETERMINING THE CAUSE OF DEATH

One of the next tasks of the forensic pathologist is to determine the medical cause of death. This is determined by the autopsy

Goals and Purpose of the Investigation

1. To help and serve the living
2. To seek the truth objectively, intellectually, and without bias or emotional coloration
3. To document guilt and protect the innocent
4. To determine the identity of the deceased
5. To determine the medical cause of death
6. To determine the manner of death

examination and the toxicology (from the Latin *toxicum* = "poison"). The toxicologist examines samples of tissues obtained during the autopsy to determine what drugs (legal and illegal) or poisons are in the body, as well as their quantity and location (in which organ or body fluid such as blood, urine, or gastric contents). The cause of death usually reflects the physical findings of the autopsy, such as a fatal disease or process (such as hemorrhage, starvation, or exposure) that caused the death of the individual. The cause of death helps to answer the question of why death occurred.

DETERMINING THE MANNER OF DEATH

The next goal of the forensic pathologist is to determine the **manner of death** (MOD), which indicates how death occurred. There are five possibilities for how death occurred:

1. Natural
2. Accident

3. Suicide
4. Homicide
5. Undetermined

A natural manner of death refers to a medical problem such as a heart attack or stroke that caused the death of the person. An accident is the result of an unexpected, unforeseen, and unintended fatal event. A suicide (from the Latin *sui* = "self" and *cidium* = "killing") is the intentional taking of one's own life. A **homicide** (from Latin *homo* = "man" and *cidium* = "killing") results from the intentional killing by another person. When the cause of death or the circumstances surrounding the death cannot be explained, the manner of death is classified as undetermined. If, at some later date, additional information becomes available, the undetermined manner of death can be reclassified. The door is always open for additional evaluation.

As part of the determination of the manner of death, the forensic pathologist must identify the **proximate cause of death**. Definitions for the proximate cause of death can vary depending on judge, jurisdiction, and individual opinion. However, the proximate cause of death is usually defined as the initial incident or act that set into motion a series of foreseeable interconnected events that led to the person's demise.

Here is an example of proximate cause: a pedestrian is struck by a car, accidentally. The driver stops, calls 911, and administers first aid and resuscitation as best he can. The ambulance arrives and whisks the patient off to the hospital. No criminal charge is made and the case is viewed as an accident. The patient remains in the hospital for 9 months in and out of coma and, despite all efforts on the part of the medical and nursing staff, eventually dies of bronchopneumonia, a natural complication of his coma and confinement to bed. Although the immediate medical cause of death in this case is the bronchopneumonia,

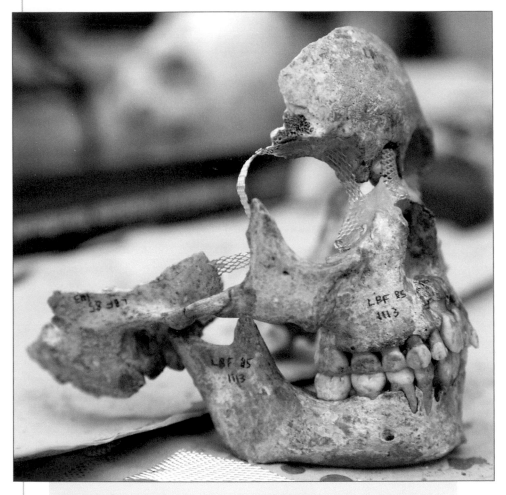

FIGURE 3.1 Forensic anthropologists rebuild human skulls when there are no other means of identifying the victim. The face is then reconstructed digitally or with modeling clay, in the hopes that the corpse will be positively identified.

the proximate (or underlying) cause of death is the injury (or injuries) the patient suffered from being struck by the automobile that put him in the hospital and eventually led to his bronchopneumonia (by virtue of his being immobilized and confined to his bed). The concept of proximate cause is best understood by the phrase, "*but for*." *But for* the automobile accident, the patient would not have suffered the injuries that led him to be immobilized in the hospital bed that led to his demise by bronchopneumonia.

4

The Autopsy

The autopsy (from the Greek *autopsia* = "a seeing for oneself" + *auto* = "self" + *opsis* = "sight") is the final medical examination a patient will undergo (unless a body is re-autopsied for any reason). The pathologist who performs the autopsy must not only answer the questions surrounding the cause and manner of death, but must also be able to explain everything else that was found in the autopsy. The additional findings help the family of the deceased understand what other medical conditions were present, which may help them cope with the loss of a loved one and may explain other symptoms or behaviors that were otherwise unexplained or poorly understood. It may also serve the family members to know if there was anything hereditary that played a role in the death that they should know about.

An autopsy is a meticulously performed procedure that is much more extensive than any kind of surgery done on a living person and consists of two parts: an external and an internal examination. Each part is performed in exactly the same way, in the same sequence, so that nothing is overlooked.

THE EXTERNAL EXAMINATION

The external examination consists of a head-to-toe detailed inspection of the body, including the hair of the scalp, the color of the eyes, the teeth and oral cavity, the neck, chest, abdomen, external genitalia, upper and lower extremities, and back. All tattoos, scars (surgical and otherwise), deformities, and injuries are noted. If there are stab wounds or gunshot wounds, these are also described, and their positions on the body noted. All findings usually are documented not only in the final written autopsy protocol but also by photographs with a ruler in the picture to demonstrate the size and shape, and also a label with the case number, the date, and the patient's name.

THE INTERNAL EXAMINATION

The autopsy incisions are then made. In men, a Y-shaped incision is made, starting at each shoulder, converging at the center of the chest, and then extending down to the pubic area (just above the genitalia). In women, the upper portion of the Y is made starting beneath each breast, forming a T-shaped incision.

The upper portion of the Y or T is dissected upward to expose the neck organs: the trachea, the thyroid, and the parathyroid glands. The neck organs are then removed, examined, and dissected. In forensic pathology, special attention is given to the muscles of the neck and to the hyoid bone, a small U-shaped bone at the base of the tongue. In some cases of strangulation, this bone is broken. The major arteries of the neck, the carotids, are preserved for the funeral director who might want to use these for purposes of embalming.

The skin of the chest is then peeled back to expose the rib-cage. The ribs directly next to the sternum (the breastbone) are cut, either with a vibrating saw or a scissor-like rib cutter. In

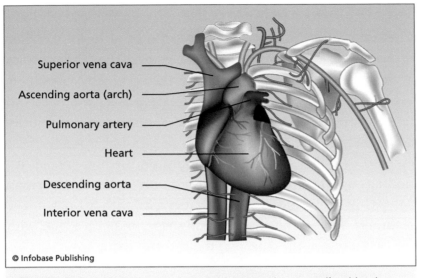

Superior vena cava

Ascending aorta (arch)

Pulmonary artery

Heart

Descending aorta

Interior vena cava

© Infobase Publishing

FIGURE 4.1   During an autopsy, the heart and surrounding blood vessels and arteries are carefully examined. In this illustration, the pericardium, the dense fibrous membrane that covers the heart, has been removed.

younger individuals, the sides of the ribs are still cartilaginous and have not yet turned to bone, so they are easily severed with a scalpel. When the ribcage is removed, the chest (pleural) cavity containing the lungs and the heart is exposed. These cavities are examined for the presence of fluid, blood, or tumor. The **pericardium** (from the Greek *peri* = "around" and *kardium* = "heart"), a fibrous sac that encloses the heart, is opened. The heart is then exposed and removed (Figure 4.1). Pulmonary blood vessels are examined for the presence of blood clots (emboli), which can cause death. The heart is removed, dissected, and weighed. The four heart valves (pulmonary, aortic, tricuspid, and mitral) are examined and measured. The heart has four chambers, two ventricles that pump the blood out of the heart into the arteries, and two atria (singular: atrium) that receive blood from the veins.

The thickness of the heart muscle of each ventricle is measured and the heart is examined for the presence of scar tissue, indicating an old heart attack or hemorrhage, or discoloration indicating a more recent attack. The coronary arteries are dissected and examined. These are like pipes that bring oxygenated blood to the heart muscle for nourishment. If there is **arteriosclerosis** and the wall of one or more of the blood vessels is calcified or the **lumen** (the space within the blood vessel where the blood flows) is narrowed by plaque or occluded by a blood clot, the blood will not be able to flow to the heart muscle and this can be a cause of death. This is commonly referred to as a heart attack. If the blockage of blood to the heart results in the death of the heart muscle, it is referred to as a **myocardial infarction**.

Each lung is weighed and dissected. The entire respiratory tract (the tubes through which air flows) from the trachea (windpipe) to the bronchi are dissected and examined for any kind of blockage or tumor. The pulmonary arteries are also dissected and examined for any kind of obstruction. The lung tissue is also examined.

Next, the abdomen is opened and the peritoneal cavity that houses all of the abdominal organs is exposed. The peritoneal cavity is also examined for excess fluid, blood, or tumor. The small intestines (duodenum, jejunum, ileum) and the large intestine (colon) are then removed. Following removal of the intestines, the remaining abdominal organs (viscera) are viewed. The liver, spleen, kidneys, and adrenals are each removed, weighed, examined, and dissected. The esophagus is dissected from the surrounding diaphragms and removed with the intact stomach and pancreas. After the stomach is opened, its contents are carefully examined and described. As previously noted, this provides a clue as to when the last meal was taken and what it was. It may also provide some information regarding the postmortem interval—

the time of death. If there are pills in the stomach, ulcers, or a reddening irritation of the lining, these must also be noted. A toxicological examination of the stomach contents is performed to determine the presence of drugs or poisons.

Next, the pelvic organs are removed. In the male, this consists of the prostate, in the female, the uterus with its cervix and attached fallopian tubes and ovaries. At this point in the dissection, the abdominal and pleural cavities are empty and the remaining ribs along the sides and the back of the body as well as the vertebral column can be inspected. If it is necessary to remove the spinal cord, it is done at this time by cutting into the vertebral column with the vibrating saw.

The next part of the body to be examined is the head. Incisions are made into the scalp behind each ear and extended around the back of the head under the hairline. The scalp is then pulled forward in front of the face, exposing the top of the skull. After the autopsy, when the scalp is put back together, the sutures are hidden by the hair and cannot be seen when the body is viewed at the time of the funeral.

Using the vibrating saw, the skull is cut in a circular fashion and the top of the skull (calvarium) is removed. Now the membranes that surround the brain (**meninges**, from the Greek *meninx* = "membrane") are visible and can be assessed for infection, fluid, hemorrhage, or tumor. There are three sets of meninges (Figure 4.2). Lying just beneath the internal surface of the skull is the outer meninx or **dura mater** (from the Latin *dura*, the feminine form of *durus* = "hard" and *mater* = "mother"), a firm, tough, and fibrous membrane that covers the outside of the brain. If there is a hemorrhage due to trauma between the dura mater and the skull, this is known as an **epidural hemorrhage** (from the Greek, *epi* = "upon" or "on top"). If the blood lies below the dura mater, this is called a **subdural hemorrhage** (from the Latin *sub* = "under"). Covering the brain, directly below the dura

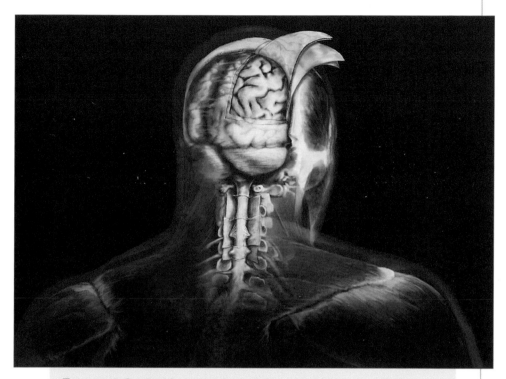

FIGURE 4.2 In this posterolateral view of the brain, membranous sheets called meninges protect the brain and spinal cord. The outer layer, known as the dura mater, is thick and tough, while the middle layer, known as the arachnoid membrane, is soft and spongy and has a web-like appearance.

mater, are two filmy, thin, transparent membranes, the **arachnoid** (from the Greek *arakhne* = "spider" + *-oid* = "-like") and the barely visible **pia mater** (from the Latin *pia* = "tender"). The two membranes are usually referred to as the **leptomeninges** (from the Greek *leptos* = "fine, thin").

The brain is examined, described, and weighed after it is removed. The membranes of the brain, the dura mater and the leptomeninges, are also examined. The brain may be dissected at this time or it may be saved for approximately 3 weeks in a 20%

solution of formaldehyde for examination by a neuropathologist after it becomes firm and easier to dissect.

FINAL STAGES OF THE AUTOPSY

At the end of the autopsy, samples of blood, urine, kidney, liver, brain, bile, and gastric contents are collected and saved for toxicological examination. Samples of each organ are also saved in a 10% solution of formaldehyde (also called formalin) to be processed for microscopic examination.

The organs and tissues that had been removed are returned to the body cavity and the incisions are sutured. At this time, the forensic pathologist lists all of the findings in a section of the autopsy protocol known as the **provisional anatomic diagnoses**. If the cause and manner of death are readily apparent, these can be listed in the autopsy protocol and on the death certificate. If the determination of the cause and manner of death are not immediately apparent, the forensic pathologist will sign a provisional death certificate as either "pending further studies" or "pending further studies and police investigation." If the cause of death is apparent, such as multiple and extensive injuries, and only the circumstances are as yet unknown to determine a manner of death, the forensic pathologist may sign the death certificate and list the cause or causes of death and then add "circumstances pending police investigation (CPPI)."

Following the police investigation and the toxicology and microscopic examinations, the forensic pathologist may issue an amended death certificate listing the final cause and manner of death.

Medical Examiner Cases

5

The medical examiner and forensic pathologist investigate all cases that appear to be related to three of the five manners of death: accident, suicide, and homicide.

One of the questions that almost always arises is: why perform an autopsy in an "obvious" case? Someone is struck by a train and is mangled. The cause of death is "obvious." A woman is brought into the morgue with a carving knife in her chest. The cause of death is "obvious." A man is cut down in a hail of bullets from an array of weapons fired by police officers. This is also an "obvious" death. A young woman falls to her death from the roof of a building. The case is "obvious." A worker is crushed by a machine—another "obvious" case.

The answers to this and similar questions is that *there is no such thing as an "obvious" case.* Did the person who was struck by the train commit suicide or was it an accident? Was he dead *before* he was struck by the train? Did the woman with a knife in her chest commit suicide or was she murdered? Was she pregnant? Was she raped? Was the man who was "cut down" by police bullets on drugs? Did he really pose a threat to the police officers that provoked the lethal force? How did the man who was crushed by a machine happen to die? Was he on drugs? Was there a defect in the machine, a previously undiscovered occupational hazard? Did he have a heart attack *before* falling into the machine? *There is no "obvious" case.* A death due to an automobile collision may truly have been an accident. However, people bent on suicide have used their automobiles as a final weapon and have driven into other cars and vehicles, trees, bridge abutments, and have stopped at railroad crossings while a train was barreling through. Did someone tamper with the automobile in order to murder the driver? An automobile fatality is not an accident until the results of the autopsy and the police investigation indicate that it actually was an accident.

MAKING DETERMINATIONS BASED ON EVIDENCE

In cases where an automobile fatality involves a car that slams into an abutment (or even another car), several clues to the driver's intent can be determined by the autopsy and the police investigation. Did the deceased leave a note? Was there an insurance policy with a suicide exclusion clause (some policies actually will pay benefits after a death by suicide but only after the insurance policy has been in force for two years)? Did the deceased have any pressing problems such as financial difficulties, an impending divorce, or other major stresses? Did the deceased talk about death or suicide with others?

In the autopsy examination, the toxicology report also becomes significant. What drugs (for example, tranquilizers or other antidepressants) were in the body of the deceased—and in what amounts? If the deceased was supposed to be on antidepressants or tranquilizers and none were found in his or her body; that may also be important. Was the deceased driving while under the influence of alcohol? Did the deceased suffer from a potentially serious or possibly lethal or painful disease that may have contributed to the crash?

One of the most important clues in this type of autopsy is not found in the body of the person but on the shoes. Often, at the time of impact, the pedal of the car leaves an imprint on the bottom of the shoe the deceased was wearing (Figure 5.1). Police investigators will retrieve the accelerator and brake pedals from the car. Comparison of the imprint on the shoe will determine whether his or her foot was on the accelerator or brake pedal at the time of impact. Naturally, an imprint matching the accelerator pedal and the lack of tire marks on the road would be highly

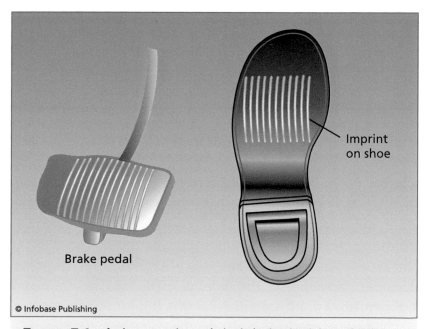

Imprint on shoe

Brake pedal

© Infobase Publishing

FIGURE 5.1 A shoe can play a vital role in the death investigation following an automobile accident. The examiner matches either the brake or accelerator pedal with the imprint embedded in the sole of the shoe in order to determine whether the fatality was a result of an accident or suicide.

significant for a determination of suicide or, perhaps, indicate that the driver fell asleep before the impact. Drugs and alcohol and a complete medical history (particularly of disorders such as insomnia or narcolepsy) or a social history of a job that required long and extended hours (such as a long-distance truck driver) may also be of help.

TYPES OF CASES THAT REQUIRE A MEDICAL EXAMINER

In addition to these "obvious" types of cases and the other types already discussed, the forensic pathologist must investigate any death that is sudden, unexplained, or unexpected. This is the type of death that is described as a "bolt out of the blue" or a "total shock." The person dies without any significant medical history or treatment and for no known reason.

Other types of cases involve deaths in children and babies, including and especially the **sudden infant death syndrome** (**SIDS**). The hallmark of this entity is a full and complete, meticulously performed autopsy that is devoid of any positive finding such as infection, injury, birth defect, or poison. In a case of SIDS, the autopsy (and total body X-rays) and all of the ancillary studies are negative. The diagnosis of SIDS is largely a diagnosis of exclusion with some constant and minor observations such as petechial (discrete pinpoint) hemorrhages sometimes seen in the conjunctiva of the inner eyelids and the surfaces of the lungs and thymus. Theories abound as to the cause of SIDS, but the cause and mechanism of death are still unknown. It is for this reason that the manner of death is usually diagnosed as "undetermined."

Cases of SIDS by definition exclude the **battered child syndrome**, in which many injuries of varying age are found, such as old hemorrhages (black-and-blue spots) and both recent and healed fractures of the extremities and sometimes of the ribs. The battered child type of case is also found in abused elderly people. These cases are referred to as **elder abuse**.

One of the hallmarks in the investigation of battered child syndrome is the tendency of the parent, caretaker, or other person to admit that the child suffered some sort of trauma but to contend that the trauma was trivial. They will admit to a fall from a sofa, chair, or bed onto a floor covered by a rug. The autopsy usually demonstrates that the violence was much more forceful and much more severe than merely a minor incident. This discrepancy between the story provided by the person supplying the information and the injuries (old and new) found at autopsy become very important in raising the degree of suspicion.

Although some children and babies are murdered out of spite during a domestic dispute or an ugly divorce, most are killed because of anger or frustration on the part of the parent or caregiver. Some are killed by mentally unbalanced people who hear voices, sometimes the voice of God or Jesus or some other deity, commanding them to sacrifice their child. In these cases, the murder may be performed as a ritual with various candles and religious objects that form a major part of the crime scene.

Unfortunately, there is an additional abuse suffered by the very young and the very old: **neglect**. This type of death includes malnutrition, dehydration, exposure to the elements by failing to supply adequate and clean apparel (especially coats and blankets during winter), or necessary heat or air conditioning. It also includes any failure by a caretaker to provide prescribed and other necessary medications. Included in this type of abuse are the religious beliefs of a caretaker or parent who refuses to seek medical attention and medications, including necessary blood transfusions for the person under their care. The victims of this abuse may not share these religious convictions or may be too young to express their own desires.

There is often a psychological benefit sought by a person who is ill, especially with a serious illness or someone who has undergone surgery. Relatives and friends show attention, love, and sympathy that the person has perhaps never known before. Some people go out of their way to become ill or even feign illness. This goes beyond simple malingering (pretending to be ill to avoid duty or work). Many of these people seek out surgeons and convince them that they are in dire need of major surgery. They do this in an effort to get attention and sympathy. People with this psychological make-up suffer from a psychological disorder known as **Munchausen syndrome** (named after Baron Karl Friedrich Hieronymus von Munchausen [1720–1797], a German soldier known for telling fantastic stories about his adventures as a hunter, sportsman, and soldier). However, there is another version of Munchausen syndrome in which a parent (usually a mother) suffocates a child and alleges that it is a case of sudden infant death syndrome. Often, they succeed and they reap the attention and sympathy of being a grieving parent because their baby has just died. Because this person elects to do something to someone else to achieve this attention, this version is known as **Munchausen syndrome by proxy**. Suspicion of Munchausen syndrome by proxy is raised when there is a pattern of multiple deaths in a single family. The killing of a baby is called **infanticide**.

One of the major decisions a pathologist must face in diagnosing the death of an infant is whether the baby was born with a **congenital defect**. There are many and varied chromosomal defects that can cause death, such as the inborn errors of metabolism in which the infant lacks certain enzymes that aid in the digestion of food. Generally, this is known as a **failure to thrive**. The dilemma is whether the death resulted from a disease process or neglect. Other congenital defects such as bleeding disorders can lead to a misdiagnosis of child abuse. Congenital heart disease and other major anatomic malformations are usually discovered during the autopsy.

Additional cases requiring the investigation of a medical examiner include any death that occurs in a workplace, judicial executions, deaths in the military, deaths of people in police custody or in prisons, and possible drug overdoses (whether the drugs are legal or illegal and whether or not the person has a history of drug addiction). Drug overdoses would also include alcohol overdoses and poisonings, usually seen in young people who are either involved in a dare, fraternity or sorority hazing, or just showing off. Death investigations may also be indicated in persons who are to be cremated, if there is any suspicion that the cremation was being done to hide a murder.

A forensic pathologist may also be called upon to investigate a **cold case**—one that has not yet been solved. To gather additional evidence, the body of a deceased person who has been buried may have to be **exhumed** for further examination (Figure 5.2). Depending on how long the body has been interred and the state of preservation—which is usually dependent on proper embalming and a leak-proof (or water-resistant) coffin—valuable evidence can be obtained by an autopsy (or a re-autopsy, as is sometimes the case).

At times, the forensic pathologist may be called upon to perform autopsies on animals. In these cases, the pathologist is performing as a **veterinary pathologist**. Such autopsies are necessary in cases where the animal has attacked and possibly killed a human. In these cases, it is important to assess the teeth

FIGURE 5.2   A coffin is raised in a cemetery in Foley, Minnesota, in November 2005. The body, which had been buried for 50 years, was exhumed in order to investigate a possible homicide.

and claws of the animal and test for rabies or other diseases. In other cases, autopsies on animals are indicated when there are a number of animals that die for some unknown reason. The cause of these deaths may be due to an environmental hazard that will also pose a threat to humans.

Besides environmental threats, the forensic pathologist is often on the front line of uncovering potentially dangerous infectious diseases that may, in the worst case, herald the start of an epidemic. In this age of terrorism, the importance of a death investigation, and even at times the examination of live individuals, has taken on a new significance due to the political nature of the crime.

6

Sudden and Unexpected Deaths Due to Natural Causes

Sudden, unexpected deaths from natural causes can be quite dramatic. A young athlete suddenly collapses on the playing field in front of hundreds of fans. A woman in the hospital, sitting up in bed gasps in mid sentence and falls back into her pillow. A man and his wife are walking on the street when he falls on the sidewalk and is dead at the scene. A man collapses while shoveling snow from his driveway. During a quiet meal at a restaurant, a man falls forward, his face hits the table and he is dead on the spot. What are some of the causes of these deaths? In all of these cases, the autopsy is central to solving the mystery.

WHEN THE CARDIOVASCULAR SYSTEM FAILS

Many of these deaths result from problems with the cardiovascular system. A blood clot in a major coronary artery completely cuts off circulation to the heart. A blood clot in the popliteal vein (behind the knee) breaks off and follows the path of blood, entering the right atrium, then into the right ventricle. From there, the blood clot is pumped by the heart into the main pulmonary arteries, where it lodges and blocks the flow to the lungs.

This is called **pulmonary embolism** (from the Greek *embolus* = "stopper, plug"). Other types of embolism are not usually associated with a natural manner of death. A fat embolus usually comes from the bone marrow after a fracture of one of the long bones of the arms or legs. An air embolus enters the bloodstream usually from a lacerated lung or vein. A bullet entering the main vein of the body, the vena cava, can even become a bullet embolus.

Arteries (the blood vessels that carry the blood away from the heart) are prone to **aneurysms** (from the Greek *aneurusma*, or *aneurein* = "to dilate"). The ascending part of the aorta (the main artery of the body) leaves the left ventricle of the heart and arcs

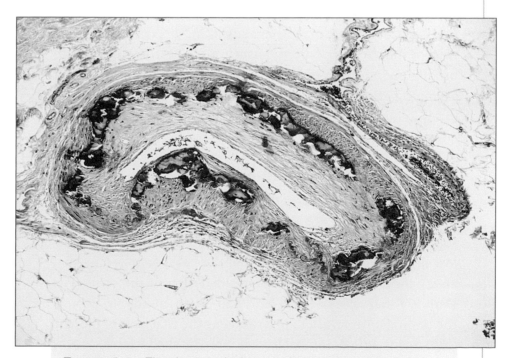

Figure 6.1 The photograph above depicts arteriosclerosis with calcification (the hardening of tissue due to calcium deposits) of the human arterial wall.

downward to form the descending aorta. Arteries, chiefly the carotid arteries, extend upward from the aortic arch to supply the head and brain. Aneurysms form from defects in the walls of arteries, either from arteriosclerosis or as a result of congenital (from birth) malformations (Figure 6.1). There are two types of aneurysms, saccular and dissecting. A saccular aneurysm is caused by a defect in or a thinning of one part of the wall of an artery. This situation is analogous to the bulge in a weakened tire, just before a blowout. Saccular aneurysms are usually found in the abdominal portion of the aorta and in the small arteries at the base of the brain. When an abdominal aortic aneurysm ruptures, death is extremely rapid because of massive internal bleeding.

Because the arteries at the base of the brain are small (especially relative to other main arteries) the bulges they produce to form saccular aneurysms are small and berry-like. For this reason, they are called berry aneurysms. These aneurysms are usually present from birth or form soon after. They are silent, asymptomatic, and deadly. A person who has a berry aneurysm rarely knows about it until it ruptures and kills.

DESIGN DEFECTS OF THE HUMAN BODY

There are two unfortunate "design defects" in the human body: the first is that there are only three main coronary arteries, each supplying a different part of the heart. When one is suddenly lost due to a blood clot, the area of the heart supplied by that artery dies. The other defect is in the design of the skull. The skull is a marvelous device, hard and tough enough to protect the brain. However, after approximately the first year of life, the skull forms a rigid, inflexible, and inelastic shell where space is at a premium. The lower portion of the brain, the brain stem, connects to the spinal cord and passes through a large opening at the base of the brain called the **foramen magnum** (from the

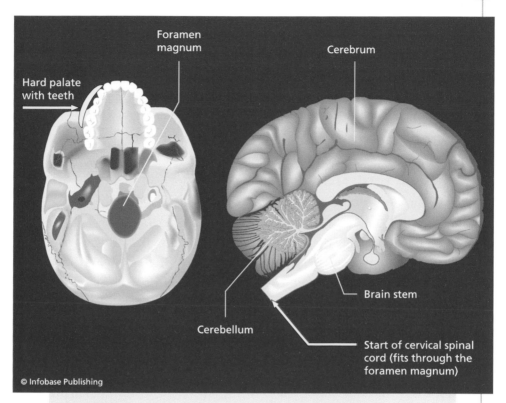

Foramen magnum

Cerebrum

Hard palate with teeth

Brain stem

Cerebellum

Start of cervical spinal cord (fits through the foramen magnum)

© Infobase Publishing

FIGURE 6.2 The foramen magnum is an open space in the underside of the skull *(left)* that houses the brain stem *(right)*.

Latin *foramen* = "opening" and *magnus* = "large"). This is the only point of "give" in the entire skull. The brain stem is the seat of most of the involuntary functions of the body such as respiration (breathing), blood pressure, digestion, alertness, and heart rate (Figure 6.2). Actually, the heart has its own nervous system that controls the beating (pumping) function. If something develops within the brain that occupies space, such as a tumor or hemorrhage, the intracranial pressure increases dramatically and forces the brain stem into the foramen magnum, squeezing these vital centers. This lethal event is called **herniation**, and it can squeeze not only the brain stem into this tight little opening, but also the tonsillar portions of the cerebellar hemispheres. The tonsillar portions of the cerebellum are small projections on each underside of the cerebellar hemispheres that resemble the tonsils found at the back of the throat.

As the aorta leaves the left ventricle of the heart, it first assumes an upward path and then U-turns downward. The point in its upward path is called the ascending aorta, the top of the U is called the **aortic arch** and the downward portion that descends into the abdomen is called the **descending aorta**. The ascending portion of the aorta, located in the chest, is prone to the other type of aneurysm, the dissecting aortic aneurysm. In the case of the dissecting aortic aneurysm, the wall of the artery splits and the blood finds an alternate path, channeling itself between the layers of the aortic wall rather than staying where it belongs, in the lumen. Circulation of blood now occurs not only in the lumen of the aorta, but also within the wall. The back pressure of the blood gradually increases the tearing effect of the wall until it becomes so thin that it ruptures. The usual site of the breach is just before the ascending aorta exits from the pericardium and the hemorrhage occurs within the pericardial sac. Here also, space is at a premium because the pericardial sac is composed of dense, inelastic, fibrous tissue. As the pressure rises inside the pericardial sac from the bleeding aorta, the heart is squeezed until it can no longer beat and pump blood.

Other events that can produce a sudden and unexpected death include an intracerebral hemorrhage (massive stroke) and fatal cardiac arrhythmia. In this case of cardiac arrhythmia, the heart quivers and shakes instead of exerting the forceful pumping action that moves the blood on its pathway to the aorta. Also, sudden death may be a result of status asthmaticus, a severe and uncontrollable asthmatic attack and a status epilepticus, a severe and uncontrollable epileptic seizure.

Another unusual form of sudden death is called anaphylactic shock or simply **anaphylaxis**. This condition is usually provoked by an allergic, hypersensitive reaction to a foreign substance found in drugs, food, or even insect bites. Death, as in status asthmaticus, usually results from respiratory failure. Autopsy findings may reveal a prominent edema (swelling) in the larynx around the area of the vocal cords that occludes (blocks) the tracheal air passage. In status asthmaticus, the microscopic examination of this area may demonstrate not only the swelling but also infiltration by eosinophils (a type of white blood cell that usually becomes quite prominent in allergic reactions and in some parasitic infestations). At other times, there is a massive amount of pulmonary edema (fluid in the lungs) and congestion with blood. These findings are nonspecific and are found in a variety of other types of death, from drowning to **asphyxia** to congestive heart failure. Statements from witnesses and the medical history of the deceased are usually helpful in making the diagnosis.

Asphyxia/Anoxic Deaths

Anoxia (*a* or *an* = "without" and *oxia* = "oxygen") refers to an absence of oxygen. Asphyxia (from the Greek *asphuxia* = "stopping of the pulse") is one of the causes of anoxia. Anoxia can also be caused by a loss of the ability of the red blood cells to carry oxygen or by a loss of red blood cells (also called erythrocytes, from the Greek *eruthros* = "red" and from the Latin *cyta* and the Greek *kutos* = "hollow vessel"). Death from anoxia/asphyxia occurs when breathing is stopped or impeded either by mechanical, drug induced, infectious, or environmental causes. Death from these conditions can also occur as a result of problems in the **central nervous system**, including brain stem compression with paralysis of the diaphragm.

Mechanical problems come about when there is an obstruction of the upper airway, the nose, mouth, or throat. Another type of mechanical problem concerns chest compression (so-called traumatic asphyxia). This type of death occurs when a weight, such as a car, a heavy person, or a mound of earth, compresses the chest so that it cannot expand to inflate the lungs.

Smothering is due to a mechanical obstruction of the upper airway by an object such as a pillow or duct tape covering the mouth and nose. Choking is caused by an obstruction to the larynx, such as by food, vomit, blood, or a foreign body (Figure 7.1). The pharynx (food tube) that connects the back of the

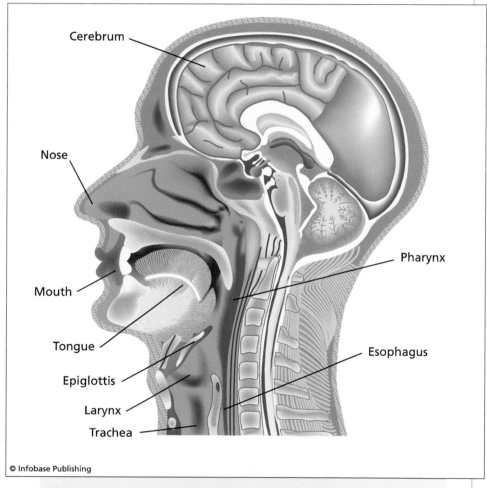

© Infobase Publishing

FIGURE 7.1   Air enters the body through the nose and mouth, then travels down the trachea toward the lungs. If the air, which contains oxygen, is obstructed before reaching the lungs, asphyxiation occurs.

mouth to the esophagus is very closely situated to the trachea (windpipe). We have all experienced the reflex of coughing and choking when something "goes down the wrong way." At times, a large **bolus** (from the Latin *bolus* or the Greek *bolos* = "lump of earth") of food material, sometimes poorly or incompletely chewed, becomes lodged in the opening of the larynx. Such a catastrophic event can cause death. The victim gags but is unable to inhale or exhale. Dr. Henry J. Heimlich, an American surgeon, devised a clever procedure to dislodge a bolus by a forceful compression of the abdomen. This sudden and forceful compression of the abdomen expels the residual air in the lungs and with it the bolus. His technique has saved many lives and has come to be known as the Heimlich maneuver.

Strangulation occurs when the outside of the neck is constricted either by the hand (manual strangulation), by a **ligature** (ligature strangulation), by an object (garrote), or by a rope (hanging). Each form of strangulation is usually associated with homicide. Hanging has also been associated with suicide and has also been regarded as an accident when used in a type of sexual perversion in which a sensation of anoxia is perceived as heightening sexual pleasure.

Strangulation and hanging leave characteristic marks on the neck. These marks are abrasion-like indentations. In cases of ligature strangulation, the marks may be circumferential, completely encircling the neck. In cases of hanging, the mark may only be present around the front of the neck and may even extend upward towards the ears, depending on the position and the type of hanging. Another characteristic often associated with strangulations and smothering is the presence of petechial hemorrhages on the face and particularly on the conjunctiva of the inner eyelids. Petechial hemorrhages are discrete bleeding points about the size of the point of a pin that result from bleeding of capillaries. These tiny hemorrhages are also seen in other conditions and are not necessarily a specific sign of asphyxia.

Environmental causes of anoxia/asphyxia include submersion (drowning), in which the breathable atmosphere is replaced by water, and asphyxia due to inhalation of a noxious gas such as carbon monoxide (CO) or hydrogen cyanide (HCN). Hydrogen cyanide has been used for judicial executions and for the mass murders performed during the Holocaust of the Nazi era in Germany. Carbon monoxide is still used to euthanize animals. Carbon monoxide results from incomplete burning and charring of carbon-based products and especially from motor vehicle exhausts. Being a colorless, odorless gas, carbon monoxide has also been a favorite means of suicide and an unfortunate type of accidental death. Fortunately, carbon monoxide detectors are commercially available. Carbon monoxide has been removed from natural gas used in the home.

Carbon monoxide kills because of its great affinity for hemoglobin, the protein material inside red blood cells that carries oxygen (Figure 7.2). When carbon monoxide binds hemoglobin, it forms carboxyhemoglobin rather than oxyhemoglobin. Hydrogen cyanide also binds hemoglobin and forms cyanhemoglobin. Other abnormal hemoglobins such as sulfhemoglobin and methemoglobin are also toxic and can be lethal. They are usually caused by the ingestion of certain drugs or toxins.

Other conditions that produce anoxia/asphyxia include any instance where other gases displace the available oxygen. Asphyxiation could occur during the inhalation of anesthetic gases such as nitric oxide during surgical or dental procedures, or in cases where these drugs were abused by healthcare workers. An example of a drug-induced asphyxia/anoxia is

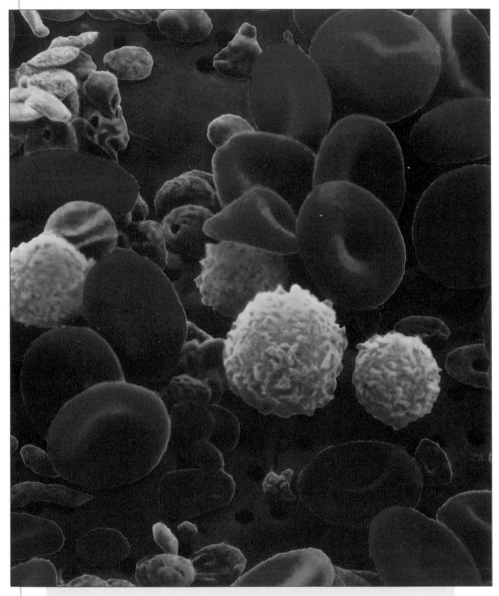

FIGURE 7.2 The above image is a colored scanning electron micrograph (SEM) of human blood showing red and white blood cells, and platelets. Red blood cells (erythrocytes) contain hemoglobin, a red pigment by which oxygen is transported around the body. Inhalation of carbon monoxide affects hemoglobin's ability to transport oxygen and can be fatal.

an overdose of a drug such as morphine, which depresses the respiratory center.

Drowning is another form of anoxic death. There are several phases involved in drowning. At first, after submersion in water, the body initiates a prompt cessation of breathing. This involuntary reflex is quickly followed by the voluntary act of holding one's breath because the victim is fully conscious and aware of the dangers of inhaling water. There is usually panic and a desperate effort to swim or to float to the surface knowing full well that if this is not possible, the result will be death. A person in good physical condition can probably hold their breath for about one minute, possibly even longer, but there is a limit (usually under two minutes). After this, another involuntary reflex occurs and the victim gasps for

Judicial Executions

In judicial executions, almost all of the various traumatic means of death have been used, including hanging, electrocution, strangling, decapitation, shooting (from a firing squad), asphyxiation with poison gases and, most recently, lethal drug injection. It is considered medically unethical for a physician to assist in a judicial execution, even to the extent of pronouncing death or inserting the intravenous needle because of one of the basic tenets of medicine: *primum non nocere* (first do no harm). However, it is not unethical, and in fact may be mandatory in jurisdictions that allow capital punishment, for a forensic pathologist medical examiner to perform an autopsy on a state-sanctioned homicide.

air. At this moment, enormous quantities of water are inhaled and swallowed. A choking cough reflex may be set up which leads to further discomfort, terror, and the inhalation and swallowing of more water. As the victim loses consciousness, the water filling the lungs oozes out of these organs into the pleural cavities (the spaces in the chest that house the lungs). If the drowning occurs in freshwater, the red blood cells in the body, which normally transport oxygen, may undergo a massive destruction (**hemolysis**). As the body fills with water, additional water may begin to leach into the abdominal (peritoneal) cavity and into the pericardial sac.

The autopsy in cases of drowning is usually able to demonstrate the watery fluid found not only in the lungs, but also in the stomach (from being swallowed). Sometimes, fluid is found in the body cavities, such as the pleural and peritoneal cavities. Other features of drowning include wrinkling of the skin of the hands called **immersion changes** or washer woman's hands (Figure 7.3). The petrosal bones, located inside the base of the skull, houses the middle and inner ears. These bones usually become extremely congested, possibly due to the pressure change caused by being underwater. As noted, the blood hemolyzes (the red blood cells swell until they burst) and paints the inner surface of blood vessels with a pink color.

As previously mentioned, decomposed bodies from an aqueous environment are called wet floaters in contrast to the decomposed bodies found on land (dry floaters). Wet floaters can be further classified as to whether they were found in salt water or freshwater, mainly by odor and by the feedings and presence of marine life such as crabs and other animals that feed on the body.

The main question confronting the forensic pathologist is: did the victim actually die of drowning? Merely finding a human body submerged or floating in the water does not

FIGURE 7.3 At left is a dismembered hand that showed severe wrinkling of the skin due to long-term submersion in water. There was also skin slippage *(right),* which allowed the thumb to be stretched over the pathologist's gloved hand and fingerprinted for identification.

necessarily indicate drowning. If a person had a massive and lethal heart attack or stroke while swimming, or experienced some other natural catastrophic event, the cause of death may not be drowning or asphyxia due to submersion. If a body was dumped into water after being murdered by a stabbing or shooting, this also does not constitute a drowning.

8 Violent Deaths Through Physical Injury

Deaths due to physical injury include the following:

1. Blunt-force injuries
2. Penetrating injuries, such as by bullets, knives, and other objects, including bomb blasts
3. Electrical injuries
4. Thermal injuries, including exposure to heat, cold, and fire

Blunt-force injuries are usually caused by an object striking the body. Sometimes, as in the case of a fall from a height, it is the body that is moving before it comes into contact with a blunt object, such as a cement sidewalk. In other cases, it is the object that is moving, such as a hammer blow that contacts a stationary head. In other cases, such as in automobile fatalities, both the body and the object are moving, usually in opposite directions.

Blunt-force objects usually cause contusions of the soft tissues (Figure 8.1). This is also known as a bruise or a black-and-blue mark (black and blue because of the hemorrhage beneath the skin). At times, the object striking the skin can leave a telltale

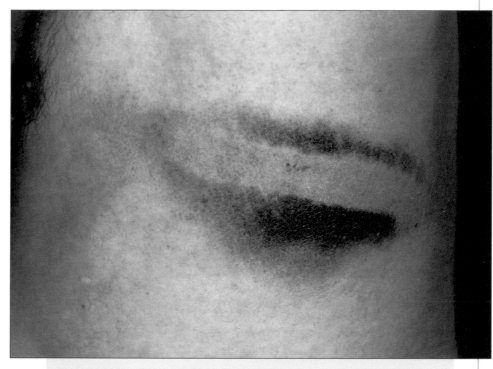

FIGURE 8.1 The photograph above shows the fractured ribs and severe bruising of a man assaulted with an iron bar.

mark or pattern known as an imprint contusion. The imprint can often be a clue to determine what object caused the injury and made this mark.

If the force is great enough, the skin may actually tear and produce a **laceration**. This type of injury may be seen anywhere on the skin as well as in the internal organs. One of the characteristic injuries caused by a blow to the mouth involves a laceration of the frenulum, the delicate membrane underneath the center of each lip (upper and lower). This is a very delicate membrane and prone to this characteristic injury.

Blunt-force injuries can also produce fractures of bones. These fractures may be of the greenstick variety (usually in young people with flexible bones). This type of fracture is like the break of a green stick (that is, there is only a crack and no separation of the parts). A comminuted fracture occurs when there is actual separation of the bones and splintering of the edges. An open or compound fracture is a serious injury in which the broken bone actually breaks through the muscle mass and the overlying skin. An avulsion is a blunt-force injury that tears the flesh from the bone or rips an eye from its socket. Fractures of the extremities may be so severe that a portion or even the entire extremity is torn from the body. This is known as a traumatic amputation. The separation of a joint is called a dislocation. When combined with a fracture, it is known as a fracture–dislocation.

Fractures of the skull are the most lethal. As previously noted, skull fractures can produce epidural hemorrhages. If the brain itself is injured, by contusion or laceration, it can produce a sub-dural hemorrhage or a hemorrhage within the **parenchyma** (the specialized tissues of the brain).

In automobile accident fatalities, there are characteristic blunt-force injuries. One type of injury, suffered by the driver, is the so-called **steering wheel injury**. Much more prevalent in the days before seatbelts and airbags, the steering wheel injury could easily be recognized by the imprint of the steering wheel that occurred at the time of impact when the driver was thrown forward against the steering wheel. This impact often produced fatal injuries with the associated fractures of the sternum (breast-bone) and the ribs. Another characteristic blunt-force imprint is the **seatbelt injury**. Seatbelts have been shown to protect a person from the effects of a car crash, but they can also leave a mark and create injuries of their own.

Another unique injury of motor vehicles is known as a **dicing injury**. Dicing injuries consist of multiple small abrasions and lacerations, particularly on the face, caused by the shattering of the side window glass of cars. This type of glass is known as

tempered glass. These are superficial injuries and not life threat-
ening, as would be the case if regular glass panes were used.

Other characteristic injuries occur when a car strikes a pedestrian. The force of the bumper can fracture the tibia or the fibula,
(the leg bones between the knee and the ankle). This is known
as a **bumper fracture**. If the pedestrian is run over by a car or
other vehicle, an imprint of the tire can often be seen either in
the clothes or on the skin. In hit-and-run homicides, it is very
important to collect bits of glass and paint chips from the victim
or crime scene. Analysis of these can often lead to the identification of the type, make, and year of the vehicle.

Blunt forces applied to the chest can create devastating injuries. These are known as flail chest injuries. In this type of injury,
the ribs are broken in many areas and the sharp edges can pierce
and lacerate the lung. The pleural cavities that house the lungs
have a negative pressure. This allows the lungs to expand and
contract during respiration when the diaphragms contract and
relax. If the lungs are injured, air can escape from the lungs into
the pleural cavity. When this happens, the negative pressure in
the chest cavity becomes positive and the lung collapses in incre-
ments with every breath. The presence of air in the chest cavity
is known as a pneumothorax (from the Greek *pneuma* = "wind,
breath"). If blood from a bleeding lung fills the chest cavity, this
is known as a hemothorax (from the Greek *haimo* = "blood"). If
there is a combination of blood and air in the chest, this is known
as a hemopneumothorax.

In motor vehicle and especially in motorcycle fatalities, almost
any bone, including the hard and sturdy pelvis can be broken
when the force is great enough. This force greatly increases with
speed and especially in head-on collisions.

A glancing or scraping blow to the skin produces a superficial
injury known as an **abrasion**. The most common example of an
abrasion is the superficial injury to the skin of the knee caused

by a fall. Sometimes an abrasion is combined with a contusion. Linear, superficial abrasions, usually caused by sharp objects such as fingernails, are known as scratches.

Superficial injuries to the skin by sharp objects such as a knife or a broken glass produce an incised wound or a "cut." This injury must be differentiated from a laceration caused by a blunt object. In the case of a laceration, the edges of the skin are torn

The Crime Scene

It is always advantageous for the pathologist to visit the crime scene of a possible homicide. By visiting the scene and actually seeing the position of the body and the pattern of injuries to the deceased and the arrangement of objects in the surrounding areas, the forensic pathologist can put the pieces of the puzzle together and attempt to reconstruct the circumstances that led to the event. The autopsy becomes a major item in the solution of this puzzle.

Crime scenes may be indoors or outdoors. The death may have occurred at the scene or the body may have been "dumped." The crime scene may be untouched since the crime was committed or it may have been contaminated by the untrained or the unwary. The murderer may have intentionally altered the scene in an effort to mislead investigators or make a statement, usually a defiant one. A crime scene altered in this manner is said to have been staged.

The first police officer to arrive at the scene makes the initial evaluation before contacting the homicide department. Once the homicide department and the medical examiner's office have been contacted, the main job of the first officer on the and ragged. Sometimes there are intact areas of skin bridging the injury. In the case of the incised wound, the edges are sharp and regular. The wound is usually superficial. Deeper wounds caused by sharp objects are known as stab wounds. Often the shape of the object that made the stab wound can be assessed by squeezing the edges of the separated skin together. If one side is blunt and the other sharp, the wound may well have been caused by a

scene is to protect the scene and maintain its purity. As the authorized personnel (the homicide detectives, crime lab technicians, photographer, and medical examiner) arrive, this officer notes their name, their rank or specialty, the time of arrival, and the time of departure for each person entering the scene.

The medical examiner's focus is mainly on the body. What is the position of the body? What clothes are on the body and are they intact, dirty, torn, or rearranged? If there is blood, is it spattered or pooled? Detailed photographs of the body and the surroundings are critical. What is the temperature of the body? What is the ambient temperature? What injuries are visible? What is the state of rigor mortis? Are there any signs of a struggle? Does anyone know the identity, or presumptive identity, of this person?

If there are bullet wounds, the medical examiner determines where the entrance wound or wounds are. If there are exit wounds, the medical examiner notes the presence of bullet holes in the walls or other objects to help determine the position of the victim when the shots were fired. Here, the expertise of the ballistics or firearm expert is crucial.

knife. If both edges are sharp, the wound may have been made by a knife with two sharp edges, such as a stiletto. Measurements of the depth of the wound can provide an indication as to the length of the blade and the size of the penetration in the skin can provide a rough idea of the width. If the wound in the skin is circular, the penetrating object may well have been round, such as an ice pick (tool for chipping a block of ice).

Stab or slash wounds can be associated with a manner of death that is either suicide or homicide. One of the clues to differentiate between the two is the presence of either a **defense wound** or a **hesitation wound.** A defense wound is usually one or more cuts or slashes found on the arms, hands, or fingers of the deceased and are manifestations of a struggle. A hesitation wound is one of the parallel directed, superficial cuts found on the wrists or on the neck of the deceased, made by the person himself or herself. These are test slashes or cuts made as the person works up his or her courage to make the fatal stab or cut to end his or her life.

Other objects can penetrate the human body. A person thrust against a pointed object can become **impaled**. Other objects such as flying glass or shrapnel from an explosion can penetrate parts of the body. Less frequently, objects such as swords, lances, or even forks or steak knives are encountered. In homicides, chiefly among family members in domestic disputes, steak knives or even scissors or letter openers are often used to stab someone. Because these are objects commonly found around the house and their use as a weapon is not planned in advance, these household objects are often called **weapons of opportunity**.

DEATH DUE TO FIREARMS

Firearms are responsible for many deaths, including the main types of unnatural deaths: suicide, homicide, and accident. A detailed discussion of the various types and classes of firearms designed for domestic and sport use as well as those employed for military and law enforcement cannot be made within the scope of this book. Suffice it to say that there are two basic weapon types: the long weapon and the handgun. Long weapons include shotguns, rifles, and the so-called automatic assault weapons. Handguns include single-shot pistols, revolvers, and automatics, usually fired with a magazine or clip of bullets. There is also a vast array of ammunition from the frangible bullets that break up after hitting a target to the hollow point bullets that open up when hitting the target (a person or an animal) to do the most damage. The size of the bullet is measured in calibers, either in decimals of an inch or millimeters.

One of the main tasks of the autopsy examination is to retrieve the bullet (or the shotgun wadding that holds the pellets together) so they can be examined by a ballistics expert who can determine the type of firearm used and, in many cases, match the specific bullet to a specific gun. Another task is to determine not only the **trajectory** (the path taken by the bullet) of the bullet within the body, but any **entrance** or **exit wounds** that may be present. This information is extremely helpful in reconstructing the positions of the shooter and the deceased relative to each other. In the examination of the entrance wound, the presence of soot, fouling, and gunpowder residue in the skin and on the clothing helps determine that the weapon was almost in direct contact with the skin of the person who was shot. A muzzle imprint demonstrates that the weapon was in direct contact with or even pressed against the skin. Stippling of the skin consists of tiny dots surrounding the wound caused by the spray of burning sparks of gunpowder. This is often regarded as an intermediate range of fire. When the diameter and shape of the stippling is recorded, subsequent test firing of the weapon by a ballistic expert can give a closer approximation of the distance involved. If none of these features is present, the range of fire is considered a distant shot, which can vary according to the type of weapon and ammunition used. A distant shot can also be confused with an exit wound because neither displays any of the gunshot residue. Exit wounds exhibit subtleties not only in shape and size, but also in appearance. Entrance and exit wounds of the skull are characterized by the funnel shaped penetrations caused by the bullet as it passes through the two layers of bone in the skull. X-rays of the body are not only helpful in actually finding the bullet (or pellets in the case of a shotgun wound) but also in determining the path of the bullet by the trail of minute metallic fragments it leaves behind. In the case of shotgun injuries, the range of fire can be gauged and approximated by the dispersal pattern of the pellets seen on X-ray (Figure 8.2). A tight cluster indicates a close range of fire as opposed to a more dispersed pattern from a more distant

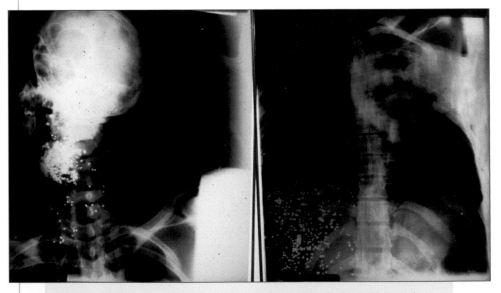

FIGURE 8.2 This X-ray reveals shotgun pellets in the head, neck, and upper chest of a shooting victim. Pathologists use the scatter pattern of the pellets to determine the distance between the shooter and the victim. The closer the shooter, the tighter the cluster.

wound. This would also correlate with the pattern of pellets seen entering the skin.

DEATH DUE TO FIRE OR ELECTRICITY

Deaths due to fires, such as house fires, are often due not only to burns, but to the inhalation of smoke and soot as well as carbon monoxide and other toxic gasses like hydrogen cyanide. These findings of inhalation of smoke and soot as well as carbon monoxide and other noxious gasses demonstrate that the victim was alive at the time of the fire. Examination of the respiratory tree (the trachea and bronchi) of someone who has died in a fire, usually shows the presence of carbon monoxide by their intense red color and the adherent soot. The lividities also show a cherry red color. Some murderers try to cover up their crime by setting fire to the room, the apartment, the house, or even the car. However, if the person was not alive at the time of the fire, there will be no carbon monoxide in the blood and no soot in the bronchi. Fires intentionally set are called **arson**. If arson leads to death, the manner of death is homicide.

Burns in the skin are classically described in degrees, depending on their severity. A first-degree burn (like sunburn) consists of a reddening type of skin irritation. A second-degree burn, usually caused by scalding with a hot liquid such as boiling water, produces blisters, small bubbles in the skin containing a clear, colorless, or slightly yellow fluid. A third-degree burn produces an actual charring or burning of the skin. The skin turns black and leathery. This is not to be confused with postmortem mummification. All degrees of burning are painful, but third-degree burns produce numbness in the area involved because all of the nerve endings are burned.

An old (and false) adage states that "lightning never strikes twice in the same place." Often it does. Lightning strikes can be deadly—and often once is enough. When a human is struck by lightning, it short-circuits the brain and heart to produce death. Sometimes there is burning of the clothes, but the most characteristic finding to indicate that a person has been struck by lightning is an arborescent or tree-like burn pattern (Figure 8.3). Lightning is a high voltage static electric charge that usually originates in the atmosphere under proper conditions. The buildup of electrical activity becomes so intense that it sparks from the sky and seeks the shortest distance to the ground. This means that it seeks the tallest object, whether it happens to be the Empire State Building, a tree, or a person.

Electrocution, once a favored means of capital punishment, kills in a similar fashion to lightning. However, alternating current does not produce the arborescent pattern seen in lightning strikes. The telltale sign of an electrocution, much like bullet wounds, is an entrance and an exit site. As in the case of lightning strikes, electric current also seeks the ground. The usual scenario is that someone touches a "live" high voltage wire. At the point of impact, there is usually a third-degree burn. As the current passes through the human body it exits at a point closest to the ground. A second burn, an exit wound, similar to the entrance site is usually found on the soles of the feet and even on the shoes. Matters can get worse and the chance of a lethal injury is markedly increased if the person is standing on a conductive material such as a metal ladder because metal is a much greater conductor of electricity than the human body.

MULTIPLE CAUSES OF DEATH

One of the main points to remember is that many deaths are due to multiple injuries or have multiple causes. There are deaths due to blunt-force injuries that also include neglect and starvation. There are murders by firearms or stabbings that may have

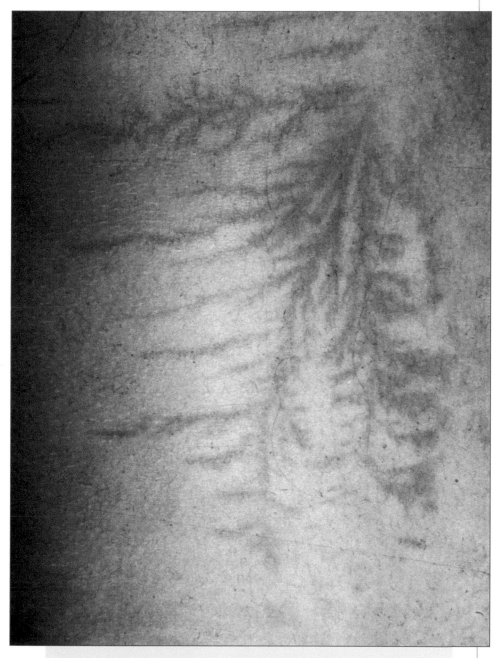

FIGURE 8.3 A tree-like burn pattern may be visible on the skin of a victim of a lightning strike.

been covered up by a house fire. Some death scenes are **staged** to falsely suggest that the death was due to an accident or to a suicide rather than a homicide. In some highly charged emotional cases, a murderer may kill a loved one and then kill himself or herself. This is termed a murder-suicide.

In the investigation of death, the forensic pathologist must view the crime scene and the autopsy with a high degree of suspicion. Rather than the "innocent until proven guilty" rule of a criminal trial, the forensic pathologist must first consider whether the case could possibly be a homicide. Evidence retrieved by the medical examiner, whether it consists of bullets or other objects, clothing or separated trace evidence (such as hair and fibers or other materials found on the body or in the clothing), must be placed in properly labeled containers and sealed (Figure 8.4). All efforts are directed to avoid contaminating the evidence by extraneous material from other cases or from those who are investigating the case, such as the pathologist, detectives, and laboratory personnel. Everyone who handles the evidence must sign or initial a receipt with the date and time. With this type of tracking system, it becomes easy to identify who handled the evidence and when it was done. Such a system is known as a **chain of custody.**

HOMICIDE

Most murders are domestic in type. The murderer and the victim either know each other or are related. Some murders occur during a robbery or other criminal activity. Other murders are perpetrated by psychopathic types of killers against people they do not know. These murderers who commit homicides with multiple victims are called **serial killers**. Often, a long time passes between killings, but sometimes individual murders happen within short periods of time followed by a longer interval in which no other murder is performed. These

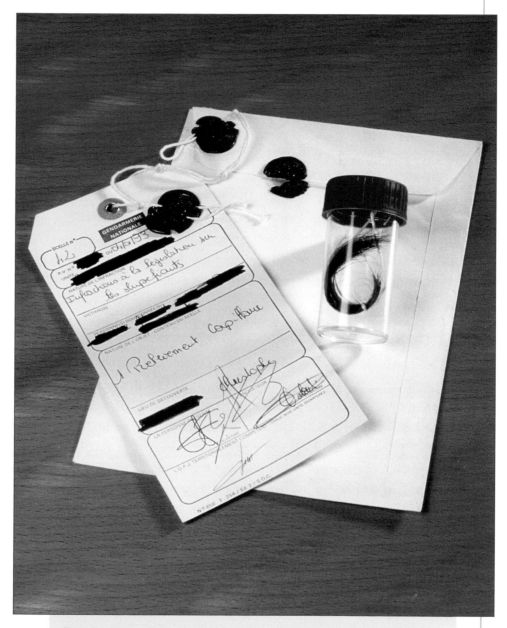

FIGURE 8.4 A vial containing a hair sample for forensic analysis rests on a record sheet sealed with wax to prevent tampering. Forensic studies on hair can place a suspect with a victim or can connect a suspect or victim to a crime scene.

murderers are known as **spree killers**. If someone murders a group of people simultaneously, this person is known as a mass murderer.

Rape is a violent crime usually perpetrated by males against females. It can also be perpetrated by males against males or even (rarely) by females against males. If it results in death, it is classified as a homicide. Usually there are other injuries that cause death such as those of stabbing, strangulation, or blunt force.

Often, a rape victim will bathe or shower after the crime because of the feeling of being "unclean" or contaminated. This, however, complicates the investigation of the crime. In addition to receiving prompt medical and psychological assistance, it is important that the victim protect any trace evidence, such as hair and fibers as well as body fluids such as saliva (from bite marks), blood, and semen for DNA analysis. This evidence can be used to identify and prosecute the rapist. Hospitals usually have an established protocol for gathering this evidence. A special kit, called a **rape kit**, is used for this purpose. Injuries are best documented by photography and diagrams.

A death due to a drunk driver (or a driver who is impaired by other drugs) who kills someone with his or her car and/or a driver who kills a person and leaves the scene of the accident is classified as a homicide. Killings by law enforcement officers are also classified as homicides. As in other homicides, it is up to the legal system to determine guilt or innocence or, in the case of a police officer, justified or unjustified. Forensic pathologists do not use an adjective such as "justified" to modify their manner of death designation especially in a police killing. To do so is for the pathologist to act as judge and jury. It also gives the appearance of a cover-up for the police department. Forensic pathologists classify the death as a homicide and let the courts determine the type.

Most legal actions have a definite and finite time frame during which an accused person must be prosecuted or have a claim filed against him or her. This time period is known as the statute of limitations. If this time frame is exceeded, no legal action can be brought to bear. However, in cases of murder, there is no statute of limitations.

9

Lawyers, the Media, and the Bizarre

Forensic pathologists must master how to deal with the press. Naturally, as in any field, there are those who thrive on media coverage and fame, and others who naturally shy away from the media and realize that it can sometimes be dangerous to have your words and opinions misinterpreted or misquoted. However, the media is ever present in criminal cases and the forensic pathologist must learn how to deal with this reality. In especially high-profile cases, there is often a "media frenzy" and the forensic pathologist may find himself or herself cornered by reporters from newspapers and television. There may be no escape and there are times when the confrontation may touch on medical confidentiality or potentially threaten a criminal investigation. The public's "right to know" may be limited solely to the cause and manner of death. Some of the details of a murder may be withheld because of the ongoing investigation. One of the important things a forensic pathologist must always keep in mind is not to guess or speculate about any part of the investigation. Any misstatement cannot be retrieved once it has left the speaker's lips and will probably come back to haunt the pathologist, especially if the speculation or guess is wrong. One of the usual places a misstatement can come back to haunt a pathologist is in the media itself. If the statement turns out to be wrong, further reports will, at best, make the pathologist look silly and, at worst, incompetent. In any case, he or she will lose credibility. Misstatements may be further explored, exploited, and second-guessed when the pathologist has to testify about the case and is faced with a grueling cross-examination by the defense counsel.

CASES THAT ATTRACT PUBLIC ATTENTION

Many of the cases that attract public attention have bizarre features. Accidents may be freakish or stupid. Add a dash of sexual interest and there is no end to the media blitz. Many bizarre deaths—especially of young males anxious to show off their bravery or entrance into "manhood," or to impress a female—often start with the words: "I dare you to . . ." or "I'll bet you can't . . ." In cases of drinking contests in bars, wild parties, and in fraternity and sorority hazings, most participants and observers view alcoholic drinks from hard liquor to beer and cocktails as merely a beverage. Ethyl alcohol (the type of alcohol found in drinks) in high quantities can and all too often cause coma and death. Other alcohols such as methyl (wood) alcohol and isopropyl (rubbing) alcohol are poisonous.

One recent craze has been the **choking game** among children and teenagers. Participants in this "game" attempt to cut off the supply of oxygen to the brain by means such as hanging or suffocation with a plastic bag. Just before they pass out, they release the noose or other paraphernalia and allow blood to fill the brain. This supposedly gives them a rush. Unfortunately, a growing number of devotees of this "game" suffer an unfortunate consequence: they die when they pass out and hang themselves.

Other cases that attract media attention involve different kinds of notoriety, from serial killings to **mass murders** to ritual or cult killings (Figure 9.1). Then, of course, there are classic cases that involve situations so unlikely or grisly as to be almost beyond belief, such as the homeless man who was electrocuted when he urinated on a subway's third rail and a

FIGURE 9.1 A medical examiner speaks to reporters about the Heaven's Gate mass suicide, in which 39 cult-members were found dead in a mansion in Rancho Santa Fe, California. Autopsy reports confirmed that the victims voluntarily ingested a lethal combination of drugs and alcohol.

suicide by a man who placed his body across railroad tracks and was severed by the train.

Another type of case is the investigation of the death of a famous person. The person may be "famous" because he or she has recently been in the news, or it may be a politician or other celebrity such as a movie or TV performer. One other situation that attracts reporters of all sorts is the mass disaster. Each jurisdiction should have a plan for dealing with a mass disaster, such as the crash of a fully loaded passenger plane, the tragedy of 9/11, explosions, and natural events such as earthquakes, hurricanes, tornados, and tsunamis. Generally, a mass disaster is viewed as a huge crime scene, or even multiple crime scenes, that should not be contaminated. The team of experts investigating the disaster must wear special hats, jackets, or identification badges to identify who they are and why they are at the site. A headquarters for the media and families of the victims is usually set up to keep up with the flow of information, maintain order, and keep family members and the press from contaminating the scene. Usually, bodies are scattered over a relatively large area, which makes the task of confining and limiting access to the scene difficult. The area or areas must be cordoned off, usually by a bright yellow tape, and protected by the police. Police are also responsible for crowd control. Inside the area, the various members of the forensic team conduct their examinations. A makeshift morgue has to be set up, with large refrigeration units. Sometimes these refrigeration units are on trucks or trains, depending on how many bodies must be processed. Markers are placed next to each body to indicate where they were found and numerous photographs and video are recorded to document the scene for the ongoing investigation. Naturally, the first and main task of the group is to locate survivors and see that they are transported to area hospitals.

As in any forensic case, one of the main tasks of the forensic pathologist, with the aid of other specialists such as forensic odontologists, is to identify the dead. A presumptive identification can usually be made on the basis of personal belongings and photo identifications such as driver's licenses.

THE MEDICAL EXAMINER IN THE COURTROOM

In a courtroom setting in criminal cases, the medical examiner is usually called to testify as a witness for the state by the District Attorney or the prosecutor (Figure 9.2). After all, the pathologist was the person who actually diagnosed the manner of death as a homicide. A forensic pathologist can also be called as an expert witness by a defense attorney. Different pathologists can voice different opinions based on the same medical evidence. Once again, it is important to remember that the forensic pathologist does not determine the "whodunit," but rather what was done and how it was done. The pathologist for the defense may offer a different scenario for the reconstruction of the crime or a different interpretation than the forensic pathologist who actually performed the autopsy.

At trial, the medical examiner will be called to the stand by the prosecutor or the district attorney. In the first part of the questioning, the pathologist is asked his or her name, address, education, professional experience, and other questions to qualify the witness as an expert in the field. This is called the direct examination. The medical examiner is then usually asked about the details of the autopsy and to explain the medical findings in layman's terminology so the members of the jury, who are likely unfamiliar with medical jargon, can understand it. The prosecutor may also ask some hypothetical questions concerning the case such as, "With these types of injuries, wouldn't you expect . . . (whatever scenario) to happen?"

FIGURE 9.2 Forensic pathologist Dr. Michael Cramer describes the wounds of sniper victim Hong Im Ballenger, during his testimony in the trial of John Allen Muhammad at the Virginia Beach Circuit Court, October 24, 2003. Muhammad was found guilty and sentenced to death for the murder of another one of his victims, Dean Harold Meyers.

After the direct examination, the defense attorney gets a chance to question the pathologist. This is called cross-examination. During the cross-examination, the defense attorney may challenge almost everything that the pathologist has said. The defense attorney may also ask hypothetical questions about the case and hope that the answers he gets will show that the case is not cut and dry, but that there is room for some doubt. It is the doubt—the "reasonable doubt" so often mentioned in television courtroom dramas—that will help his client. After the cross-examination is finished, the district attorney will have one more chance to correct any misconceptions that may have arisen during the cross examination. This is called the redirect.

Gray Areas and the Forensic Team

The practice of medicine and pathology includes certain pro-cedural rules. Every rule, however, has exceptions and that is where personal decision and experience come into play. The personal decision is not a mere "flip of the coin." A personal decision, especially of this magnitude, relies on a solid base of education (background and continuing) as well as experience and clear thinking.

This responsibility presents major problems—and major challenges—for physicians and forensic pathologists. Often, someone's life is at stake and decisions become extremely critical. In clinical medicine, a misdiagnosis of a potentially serious illness may be fatal to the patient, either because the illness without therapy may be fatal or the therapy without the illness may be poisonous. In forensic pathology, a misdiagnosis of a manner of death concerning homicide may cause untold suffering to the deceased's family, send an accused but innocent person to his death (by capital punishment), or allow a murderer to go free and perhaps strike again.

The forensic pathologist is faced with many difficult questions. Is the bullet wound in the body an entrance wound fired at a distance or an exit wound? Did a possibly lethal injury result after death or before? Were the broken ribs and lacerated liver due to faulty and excessive resuscitative procedures or were they blunt injuries and the actual cause of death? Did the deceased fall from a height or was he or she pushed? Did the deceased fire the weapon that killed him or did someone else do it? The answer to these questions may not be clear cut and the forensic pathologist has to carefully weigh all the possible evidence before coming to a conclusion.

One highly perplexing scenario is a death that occurs while a person is in the custody of police or other law-enforcement personnel. How did the death happen? Was it due to drugs and/or alcohol that made the deceased become aggressive? Was it a so-called case of excited delirium, in which the prisoner or other detained person seems to go berserk just before death for no explainable reason? Was it because the police pounced on him and created a positional or traumatic asphyxia? Cases such as these put the training and investigative skills of the pathologist to the test.

DIFFICULT CASES INVOLVING INFANTS

Faced with the death of an infant in which there are no positive anatomic, infectious, or toxicological findings, should the pathologist diagnose a smothering or a case of sudden infant death syndrome? Often there is no objective way of differentiating between the two conditions unless there is some injury to the mouth or nose or evidence is brought out by the investigation. Parents of children who die suddenly and mysteriously suffer not only from grief but also from the enormous psychological effects of pain and guilt (some berate themselves for not being more vigilant). Can it be justified to accuse them of murdering their child with a possibly erroneous diagnosis of smothering, thus adding to their psychological burden?

Another gray area is the so-called **shaken baby syndrome.** The cause and manner of death in these cases is well recognized in forensic medicine. This is a homicide usually caused by a parent or caregiver who gets frustrated and angry because of the infant's incessant crying, or because the child refuses to eat, or perhaps it soils its diaper too often for the parent or caregiver's expectations. The parent or caregiver then vents his or her frustration by shaking the baby violently.

In infants, the neck muscles are not strong enough to give full support to the relatively large head. As a result of violent shaking, the head is propelled back and forth with a great deal of force and speed. The brain of the infant, loosely housed in the skull for continued growth, is also forced to move or even rotate within the skull. This leads to what is known as shearing forces as the brain slides against the meninges. Thin-walled blood vessels tear and bleed as a result of these shearing forces. The result is a subdural hemorrhage. Sometimes the infant survives the mistreatment and the hemorrhage resolves itself spontaneously and begins to heal. Unfortunately, during this healing period, the baby may be shaken again, either by the original parent or caregiver or by someone else. In this case, a rebleeding occurs. Bleeding or rebleeding in the skull creates pressure on the brain. Because the eyes are also an anatomic part of the brain, bleeding can also occur in the area of the optic nerve (the nerve that conducts light to the parts of the brain responsible for vision). The retina, the back part of the eye, contains nerve endings and can also be injured. One of the additional signs of shaken baby syndrome are retinal hemorrhages. There may also be a skull fracture. When this occurs, it is known as a shaken baby/shaken impact syndrome.

Shaken baby syndrome is one of the biggest areas of controversy in forensic medicine. There are some who dispute the notion that there is such a thing as shaken baby syndrome; these people point out that there are other causes for subdural and retinal hemorrhages. These causes are attributed to a wide variety of possibilities, including the baby's genetic makeup, a spontaneous tendency to bleed, a vitamin deficiency, or unusual complications from a vaccination.

It is also often uncertain, from the point of view of a police investigation, who actually did the shaking. Often, the last person to have handled the child is the one accused. This person, in actuality, may or may not have been the one who shook the baby. Accusing someone (especially the last one to have been with the baby) often resembles a game of musical chairs.

THE SUPPORTING CAST

In this text, only a few of the people who make up the forensic team have been mentioned. These include the homicide detectives, the neuropathologists, the toxicologists, and the technicians in the crime lab and in the firearms and ballistics section. In addition, the forensic anthropologist may be required to determine the age, sex, and sometimes the identity of the deceased by facial reconstruction.

The main members of the forensic team are:

1. **Forensic toxicologists**: Analyze blood and tissues to determine the presence or absence of poisons and drugs.
2. **Forensic odontologists**: Identify the deceased and evaluate any bite marks that may be present.

3. **Forensic anthropologists**: Evaluate skeletal remains.
4. **Forensic entomologists and biologists**: Evaluate flora and fauna to determine the time and place of death.
5. **Forensic psychiatrists and psychologists**: Evaluate the accused perpetrator, identify behavioral profiles of the victim and/or suspect.
6. **Criminalistics**: Specialists responsible for evaluating evidence that falls in the fields of their expertise, including ballistics experts, trace evidence (hair and fiber analysis) specialists, fingerprint analysis, hematologists, and geneticists.
7. **Document experts**: Conduct handwriting and document analysis.
8. **Forensic Engineers**: Evaluate machines, vehicles, and constructions.
9. **Forensic Photographer**: Take and document images of the crime scene.
10. **Homicide and arson detectives**: Investigate the circumstances of death and arrest of suspects.
11. **Road medical examiners, emergency medical technicians (EMTs), and police surgeons**: The eyes and ears of the forensic pathologist at the scene.

One of the main members of the supporting cast is the autopsy assistant, the **diener** (German for "servant"). The diener helps the pathologist perform the autopsy, sews the body together after the procedure, and also makes sure that the specimens are labeled correctly. Another set of eyes viewing the anatomy of the deceased often proves helpful.

Of course, many unsung heroes and heroines work behind the scenes, such as clerical workers, microbiologists, histology technicians, drivers, dispatchers, and other workers who make the medical examiner's office function smoothly. Outside agencies such as the county or state health department also play a role. The forensic pathologist may be the star, but the supporting cast is often of critical significance.

Abrasion   A superficial injury to the skin caused by scraping or scratching.

Adipocere   The insoluble, wax-like residue that develops in a decomposed human body in an aqueous environment.

Algor mortis   Cooling of the body after death.

Anaphylaxis   A severe and possibly deadly allergic reaction.

Anatomic pathology   The branch of medicine that focuses on diagnosing disease through the analysis of tissue samples.

Aneurysm   A weakening of the wall of an artery. Either the wall of the artery bulges like a tire or a balloon ready to explode (a sacular aneurysm) or the artery has a defect that allows blood to flow not only within the lumen where it belongs but also to burrow a path between the linings in the wall of the artery (a dissecting aneurysm).

Anoxia   Without oxygen.

Aortic arch   The curved portion of the aorta as it leaves the heart.

Arachnoid   The spider web-like middle membrane covering the brain.

Arson   The setting of a fire with the intent to destroy property.

Arteriosclerosis   Hardening of the arteries, including deposits of cholesterol and calcium on the inner lining of the artery that impedes the free flow of blood or the deposits of calcium in the wall of the artery making it hard and brittle.

Arrhythmia   A disorder of the rhythmic beating of the heart.

Asphyxia   A lack of oxygen in the body that usually results from an interruption of breathing.

Autolysis   The breakdown of organs and tissues in the body undergoing a decompositional change.

Autopsy   Surgical examination of the body after death.

Battered child syndrome   The collection of physical injuries typically sustained by a child subjected to abuse.

Biopsy   Examination of a sample of tissue from the body.

Bolus   A mass of partially chewed food that becomes lodged in the throat or windpipe during swallowing.

Brain death   The irreversible cessation of the electrical activity in the brain.

Bumper fracture   Characteristic injury that occurs when a pedestrian is struck by a vehicle, involving breaks to the fibula, tibia, or both.

Cadaveric spasm   Phenomenon in which the muscles, particularly those of the hand, contract forcibly at the moment of death.

Cellular death   Death of the cells within an organism.

Central nervous system   The part of the nervous system made out of the brain and the spinal cord.

Chain of custody   Tracking system designed to maintain records of who handles and examines evidence during the investigation of a death.

Choking game   A dangerous fad among children and teenagers in which participants test how long they can deprive their brains of oxygen before passing out.

Cold case   A criminal investigation that has not yet been solved.

Congenital defect   A defect or disease present at the time of birth, usually a genetic disorder.

Coroner   An official responsible for investigating a death that is not the result of natural causes.

Contusion   A blunt force injury that causes bleeding. In the skin it is usually described as a bruise or a "black and blue" mark.

Criminalistics   Application of scientific techniques in the collection and analysis of evidence in a criminal case.

Cytopathology   Diagnosis of disease by examination of individual cells instead of tissue specimens.

Defense wound   Cuts or slashes found on the arms, hands, or fingers of a deceased person that are suggestive of a struggle with the person's attacker.

Deoxyribonucleic acid (DNA)   Molecule found in the nucleus of living cells that encodes the genetic information of the organism.

Dermatopathology   The study of the causes and course of skin diseases.

Dicing injury   Small abrasions and cuts, especially on the face, caused by shattered window glass due to a car crash.

Diener   Autopsy assistant; comes from the German word "diener," which means a "servant."

Dry floater   A decomposed body found on land and exposed to air.

Dura mater   The thick and dense tough membrane directly beneath the skull covering the brain.

Entrance wound   A perforating injury caused by the entrance of a foreign object, such as a bullet or a knife or even electricity into the body.

Epidural hemorrhage   Bleeding in the area between the skull and the outer layer of the membrane that surrounds the brain.

Exit wound   The injury caused when a foreign object, such as a bullet or a knife or even electricity exits the body.

Exhume   To remove a body which has been buried from the grave for an autopsy examination.

Failure to thrive   A condition in which a baby or young child does not gain weight and grow normally.

Foramen magnum   The large hole at the base of the skull where the base of the brain continues as the spinal cord, exits the skull and moves down the body through the center of the vertebral bones of the spine.

Forensic anthropologist   A physical anthropologist who evaluates skeletal remains to help determine the identification and possibly the cause and manner of death.

Forensic entomologist   A type of forensic scientist that studies the association between insects and the human corpse.

Forensic odontologist   A subspecialty of dentistry involved in postmortem identifications comparing dental X-rays taken during life with those taken after death. The forensic odontologist is also an expert in evaluating bite mark evidence.

Glossary

Forensic pathology   Subspecialty of pathology in which the main diagnostic effort is directed toward determining the cause and circumstances of death. Also known as forensic medicine.

Hematopathology   The study of diseases affecting the blood and blood-forming organs, including the bone marrow, spleen, and lymph nodes.

Hemolysis   The breakdown of red blood cells.

Hesitation wound   A parallel, superficial cut found on the wrists or neck of a deceased body, made by the person himself or herself.

Homicide   The killing of one person by another.

Immersion changes   Features of a deceased body, such as wrinkled hands and fluid within the body, that are characteristic of drowning.

Impale   To pierce with a pointed object.

Infanticide   Killing of a baby.

Jurisprudence   the study of law and the legal system.

Laceration   A blunt force injury that causes tearing of the tissues.

Leptomeninges   The almost inseparable combination of the delicate middle arachnoid (spider web-like membrane) and the transparent inner membrane covering the brain, the pia mater.

Ligature   A cord that can be used to bind a person.

Livor mortis   Purplish red discoloration of the skin of a deceased person that results from the settling of blood in the lower regions of the body.

Manner of Death (MOD)   The circumstances of how a patient died. The five possible manners of death include: natural, suicide, homicide, accident, and undetermined.

Macerated   Decomposition in a fetus that has died before birth in the sterile environment of its mother's uterus.

Marbling   A change in the appearance of the skin of a deceased person after death, characterized by a greenish discoloration around the umbilicus (navel).

Mass murderer   A person who kills several people at the same time in the same place who may or may not be known to the murderer.

Medical examiner   A physician serving as a government official that is responsible for determining the cause and manner of death in fatalities.

Meninges   The coverings of the brain inside the skull. Inflammation or infection of these membranes is known as meningitis.

Mummification   Shrinkage and drying of the skin of a deceased body that results under certain environmental conditions.

Munchausen syndrome   Psychological condition in which a person fakes the symptoms of a serious illness with the intention of gaining the attention and sympathy of others.

Munchausen syndrome by proxy   Psychological condition in which a person causes symptoms of a serious illness in someone else, usually a child, to gain the attention and sympathy of others.

Myocardial infarction   Damage to the heart muscle due to a lack of blood from the coronary artery.

Neglect   Failure to provide levels of care required to meet a dependent person's needs.

Neuropathologist   A specialist who studies diseases of the nervous system.

Parenchyma   The specialized tissues forming the substance of an organ.

Pathologist   A doctor who specializes in examining cells and tissue in order to diagnose disease.

Pericardium   The dense fibrous membrane that encloses (surrounds) the heart.

Persistent vegetative state   Condition in which a patient is unable to perform basic functions (such as speaking or following simple commands) and shows no ability to respond to his or her surroundings.

Pia mater   The transparent innermost membrane covering the brain.

Postmortem interval   Time of death.

Postmortem lividity   The settling of the blood in the body after death, which results in a blue/purple discoloration of the skin.

Glossary

Presumptive identification Preliminary determination of the identity of a deceased person on the basis of items (such as a Social Security card, driver's license, or passport) found with the body.

Provisional anatomic diagnoses A listing made of the autopsy findings made by a forensic pathologist.

Proximate cause of death The initial incident or event leading to an individual's death.

Pulmonary embolism Usually a blood clot that arises in some other blood vessel (a vein) that travels back through the heart and into the pulmonary artery, blocking it completely. This sometimes causes a dramatic sudden death if the embolism is massive and occludes both pulmonary arteries.

Rape kit Package of items used in a hospital to gather evidence (such as samples of hair, saliva, semen, and blood) that can be used to identify and prosecute a rapist.

Rigor mortis Stiffening of muscles that occurs after death.

Seatbelt injury Blunt-force injury that commonly occurs to people who have been in a car accident.

Serial killer A person who murders several people, usually complete strangers over a period of time

Shaken baby syndrome Homicide in which a young child dies as a result of being violently shaken by a frustrated or angry parent or caregiver.

Smothering Mechanical obstruction of the upper airway by an object such as a pillow or duct tape covering the mouth and nose.

Somatic death Death of an organism (person or animal).

Spree killer A person who kills several people, usually complete strangers, at different locations within a relatively short period of time.

Stage To arrange the setting where a death has occurred to make it appear that the cause of death was different from what it actually was.

Steering wheel injury Blunt-force injury that commonly occurs to the driver in a car accident.

Strangulation   Constriction of the outside of the neck by the hand or an object.

Sudden infant death syndrome (SIDS)   Unexplained death that occurs without warning in infants in which autopsy results are invariably negative.

Subdural hemorrhage   Bleeding within the membranes that cover the brain.

Trajectory   The path taken by a bullet or another object.

Veterinary pathologist   A forensic pathologist who perform autopsies on animals, usually in cases where the animal has attacked a person, to determine whether the animal carried rabies or other potentially dangerous diseases.

Wet floater   A decomposed body found in water and exposed to an aqueous environment.

Weapons of opportunity   Common objects used as the instruments of violence or murder in the "heat of the moment."

BIBLIOGRAPHY

Adelson, Lester. *The Pathology of Homicide a Vade Mecum for Pathologist, Prosecutor and Defense Counsel.* Springfield, Ill: Charles C. Thomas, Publishers Ltd, 1974.

DiMaio, Vincent J.M. *Gunshot Wounds: Practical Aspects of Firearms, Ballistics, and Forensic Techniques,* 2nd ed. Boca Raton, Fla: CRC Press, 1999.

DiMaio, Vincent J. M., and Dominick DiMaio. *Forensic Pathology.* Boca Raton, Fla.: CRC Press, 2001.

Dix, Jay. *Color Atlas of Forensic Pathology.* Boca Raton, Fla: CRC Press, 2000.

Ecker, William G.G. *Introduction to Forensic Sciences,* 2nd ed. Boca Raton, Fla: CRC Press, 1996.

James, Stuart H. (ed.), and Jon J. Nordby. *Forensic Science: An Introduction to Scientific and Investigative Techniques.* New York: Taylor & Francis, Inc., 2005.

Kobilinsky, Lawrence, Thomas F. Liotti, Jamel L. Oeser-Sweat, et al. *DNA: Forensic and Legal Applications.* New York: Wiley, 2004.

Kumar, Vinay, Abul K. Abbas, and Nelson Fausto. *Robbins & Cotran's Pathologic Basis of Disease,* Seventh Edition. Philadelphia, Pa.: Elsevier Saunders, 2004.

Mason, Ken K. (ed.), and Basil Purdue (ed.). *Pathology of Trauma.* New York: Oxford University Press, 2000.

Payne-James, Jason (ed.), Roger W. Byard (ed.), Tracey Corey (ed.), et al. *Encyclopedia of Forensic and Legal Medicine,* Vols. 1–4. Boston, Mass.: Elsevier Academic Press, 2005.

Saukko, Pekka, and Bernard Knight. *Knight's Forensic Pathology,* 3rd ed. New York: Oxford University Press, 2002.

Schneider, Arthur S., and Philip A. Szanto. *Pathology (Board Review Series),* 2nd ed. Philadelphia, Pa.: Lippincott Williams & Wilkins, 2001.

Spitz, Werner U. (ed.). *Spitz and Fisher's Medicolegal Investigation of Death: Guidelines for the Application of Pathology to Crime Investigation,* 3rd ed. Springfield, Ill.: Charles C. Thomas, 1993.

Wetli, Charles V., Roger E. Mittleman, and Valerie J. Rao. *An Atlas of Forensic Pathology*. Chicago, Ill.: American Society Clinical Pathology Press, 1999.

FURTHER READING

Bell, Suzanne. *Encyclopedia of Forensic Science*. New York: Facts On File, 2003.

DiMaio, Vincent J., and Suzanna E. Dana. *Handbook of Forensic Pathology*. Austin, Tex.: Landes Bioscience, 1998.

DiMaio, Vincent J., and Dominick DiMaio. *Forensic Pathology*. Boca Raton, Fla.: CRC, 2001.

Dix, Jay, and Robert Calaluce. *Guide to Forensic Pathology*. Boca Raton, Fla.: CRC, 1998.

Gall, John A.M. *Forensic Medicine*. New York: Churchill Livingstone, 2003.

Genge, Ngaire E. *The Forensic Casebook: The Science of Crime Scene Investigation*. New York: Ballantine, 2002.

Platt, Richard. *Crime Scene: The Ultimate Guide to Forensic Science*. New York: DK, 2006.

Walker, Maryalice. *Pathology*. Philadelphia, Pa.: Mason Crest, 2006.

Web Sites

American Academy of Forensic Sciences (AAFS)
http://www.aafs.org

American College of Forensic Examiners Institute of Forensic Science
http://www.acfei.com

Crime Scene Creatures
http://www.pbs.org/wnet/nature/crimescene/

Crime Scene Investigation: The Medical Examiner
http://www.crimelibrary.com/criminal_mind/forensics/crimescene/4.html

Dead Man's Tales
http://www.pbs.org/saf/1203/index.html

Dr. G: Medical Examiner
http://health.discovery.com/fansites/drg/drg.html

Interactive Investigator

http://www.virtualmuseum.ca/Exhibitions/Myst/

National Association of Medical Examiners Website

http://www.thename.org

Young Forensic Scientists Forum

http://www.aafs.org/default.asp?section_id=resources&page_id=young_
    forensic_scientists_forum

PICTURE CREDITS

INDEX

Index

Index

ABOUT THE AUTHOR

Dr. Howard C. Adelman received his B.A. degree from Gettysburg College and his M.D. degree from the University of Basel, Switzerland. Dr. Adelman's professional career spans more than 30 years and includes experience in all phases of pathology (anatomic, clinical, forensic, and cytopathology). He has served as the medical director of hospital laboratories, a forensic medical examiner's toxicology laboratory, and private laboratories. During this time, he has also been a private pathology consultant to the legal profession on matters ranging from death and injury investigation to medical malpractice.

In addition to serving as a forensic consultant on network and local news, Dr. Adelman has been a guest on Court TV and recognized as a medical expert in many state courtrooms. As deputy chief medical examiner of Suffolk County, New York, he investigated one of his most famous cases, the mass murder of the DeFeo family in Amityville. This case achieved notoriety not only because it was the largest mass murder ever committed on Long Island, New York, but because it became known as "The Amityville Horror," the subject of several books and a series of films. A member of the Screen Actor's Guild (SAG), Dr. Adelman's onscreen interview for the latest version of the movie *The Amityville Horror,* released to theaters in April 2005, can be seen on the DVD. He has also appeared in a documentary about the murders for the A&E network, which was broadcast in April 2006.

Dr. Adelman is married to his wife, Nancy, and has three sons, Adam, Dan, and Jeremy, as well as three daughters-in-law, Belinda, Sumi, and Samanta. He also enjoys the company of his three granddaughters, Selina, Maya, and Juno.

ABOUT THE EDITOR

Lawrence Kobilinsky, Ph.D., is a professor of biology and immunology at the City University of New York John Jay College of Criminal Justice. He currently serves as science advisor to the college's president and is also a member of the doctoral faculties of biochemistry and criminal justice of the CUNY Graduate Center. He is an advisor to forensic laboratories around the world and serves as a consultant to attorneys on major crime issues related to DNA analysis and crime scene investigation.